From Pen
to Page

a selection of writings from the
Bluegrass
Writers
Coalition

From Pen to Page
a selection of writings from the Bluegrass Writers Coalition

Copyright © 2019 by Bluegrass Writers Coalition

Published by the Bluegrass Writers Coalition, an unincorporated literary organization.

Cover design by Virginia Smith
Interior images by Michael Embry, unless otherwise noted
Editing services: Keith Hellard, Chris Helvey, Michael Embry

ISBN-13: 978-1-937671-92-1

Copyright Acknowledgements

This book is dedicated to Mark Kinnaird: poet, friend, and founding member of the Bluegrass Writers Coalition

Photo by Melanie Allbright Llontop

Contents

Kentucky River

Introduction

The vision for this volume arose during a 2018 chat over coffee between two of the founding members of the Bluegrass Writers Coalition (BWC). That original vision was ephemeral, nebulous, and only began to truly take form and shape several months later as the first submissions flowed in.

While we were hopeful that we would receive enough submissions to produce a legitimate book, we never expected so many writers here in the Bluegrass region of Kentucky to submit such a wide variety of work.

Our initial expectations were that we might get a handful of poems and a short story or two. Wow, we were wrong!! *From Pen To Page* does indeed contain a number of fine poems and some creative and powerful short stories. However, it also provides the reader with memoir pieces, creative nonfiction, novel excerpts, even photographs of Frankfort (home of the Bluegrass Writers Coalition) and the famous Bluegrass countryside that surrounds Kentucky's capital city.

This volume reveals Kentucky writers who are thoughtful and creative, and addresses a myriad of subjects: war, love, death, murder, heartbreak, family ties, avarice, beauty, childhood, fantasy, and on and on and on.

Just as the works in the volume reflect an exceptional variety of forms, formats, and subjects, the authors of these works come from a variety of backgrounds, lifestyles, and artistic sensibilities. Some of us are native Kentuckians, while others journeyed here later in life. Our ages vary from early 20s to the mid 70s and our professions vary from schoolteacher to journalist to truck driver to government worker to…

For some of the writers in this volume, this will be their first publication. For others it will be another in a long line. All the work — layout, photography, proofreading, editing — was performed by BWC members. Our collective goal was to produce a volume of good literature of great variety that readers of many different interests could enjoy. We sincerely hope you agree that we have succeeded.

Bluegrass Writers Coalition
October 2019, Frankfort, Kentucky

Floral Clock

Violets For Sergeant Schiller

Chris Helvey

A Novel Excerpt

Chapter 1
The Plaza de la Enfants

I am strolling across the Plaza de la Enfants. The sun blazes in a cloudless sky and a band plays a martial tune at the corner.

Before me a small boy is buying a balloon from the balloon man. He buys a red one, the color of fresh blood, and turns and runs back to an old woman in black who leans on her cane. She is smiling and they hold hands while a cavalcade of pigeons struts around them. The old woman and the small boy are standing in the shadow of the statue of Saint Marguerite. It is a very hot day and the wind of Paris has been still all this summer. Under my hat I am sweating and suddenly a longing to be strolling among the thick forests of

Bavaria rushes through me.

But I have business to attend to before I can go home. It has been a busy summer for me and I should be grateful. After all, not many poets can claim to have signed three contacts for their books in a single summer.

Over the years I have noticed that life seems to come at one in cycles, or tides if you will. The tides are coming in now for Karl Ernst Schiller and I should be grateful. Yet, I am tired, hot, and lonely and long for home.

As I step among the pigeons they cry out and rise in a feather-whirling mass, obscuring the sun for a moment before they angle above the old woman and the boy and the statue of Saint Marguerite. Someone, I cannot recall whom at the moment, has told me that she is the patron saint of lost children. But I am a spiritual man and not a religious one and, therefore, cannot answer for the veracity of this claim.

The little boy laughs as the birds fly by him and his laughter follows me across the Rue Rampart. The laughter seems to echo in the air. Today the air is not the same as it was yesterday, or the day before, or the week before, or the month before. There is a hollow quality to it and to the day. That quality gives me the sense that both the air and the day are fragile and that one misstep would shatter the world

At the far side of the street I turn and look back. The old woman has turned away, but the little boy still stares at me. For a moment he seems like a younger, more innocent version of myself. In unison we raise an arm and wave. Somehow it seems that I am saying goodbye to myself.

A bent little man with drooping mustaches has set up his flower cart on the curb. It is a small cart and many of the flowers do not appear particularly fresh. However, he does have a nice pot of violets. Violets have been my favorite

flower for as long as I have had memory. The first I can recall were wild ones in the woods outside of Koblenz. In the
summer I would see them, purple and cool looking, on a hot
day such as this one. My aunt often took me for long walks
in the woods. Beneath the trees it was always dark and cool,
and you felt as though you could draw a good breath. Shadows lay on the earth like soft, dark blankets. Under the pines
there were violets. I remember laughing when I saw the first
patch of violets and running to pick them. I must have been
five or six years old.

My aunt followed me. Her name was Berta. We sat
amongst the violets and picked great handfuls of them. We
both laughed so loudly that the squirrels scampered up to
the tops of the oaks. My aunt was a plump woman with a
pretty face and bad teeth. She kissed me on the mouth while
we picked the violets and touched me in special places. Then
she had me kiss her and touch her, too. She said the kisses
and the violets must be our secret. I have not thought for
that afternoon for years. I have kept the secret well. I am a
good keeper of secrets.

Chapter 2
Monsieur Aubier

As I climb the stairs I hear the lifting sounds of a violin.
It is being played by a Japanese girl who lives on the second
floor. I have seen her twice when visiting Monsieur Aubier.
Monsieur Aubier is my publisher. The girl is quite young.
She is blind and lives with her grandmother. All the tunes
she play sound blue to me. Colors are very important to me,
colors and light. Often, I see life solely in those two realms.

Blue slow dances up the stairs
In the arms of mauve
as night falls in an uneasy Paris

On the landing of the fourth floor I lean against the wall to recover my breath. For a man not yet thirty I am in deplorable condition. My days of kicking a football around and hiking the mountain trails seem to belong to a distant path, or to another man. Yet, it has been less than ten years since I left the university to strike out on my own. What, I wonder, will another ten years bring?

Behind the door to apartment 14 I hear the clutter of pans and a woman singing. She has a pleasant voice, if slightly off key. She is singing a love song that was popular thirty years before.

Behind the door to number 14 live M. Aubier and his wife, Marie. Their daughter Michelle lives there, too, when she is not visiting cousins in Burgundy. M. Aubier has been my publisher for almost seven years.

Hand raised, I pause. For the first time I notice that the door is scarred. Someone has kicked it so hard that it has splintered near the bottom and it badly needs painting. I look around me. The landing is quite tawdry. Cobwebs drape the corners and fly specks dot the single window. The wallpaper, which must at one time have been a bold blue and gold stripe, is now sadly faded. I wonder.

I knock and the singing ceases. Before I have time to wonder further I hear the latch being lifted and the door creaks open and Madame Aubier smiles at me. She has a shy smile, like a little girl. At heart, despite her years, I think she is still a little girl. I have noticed that it is impossible for some people to truly grow up.

Across the room, M. Aubier struggles to rise from his chair. When just a boy of nineteen a shell struck near him during the war. Over one hundred fragments lodged in his legs. Always I am amazed that he does not harbor a burning hatred for all Germans. In those days the doctors were not well trained. Since the war his legs have never been right. He is a remarkable man.

"Ah, Karl, come in, come in. And how is my favorite author? Sit, sit, I know you must be tired. No, exhausted after riding that awful, noisy train. Oh, how I hate loud noises."

There are not many seating choices. The chaise and most of the chairs are covered with books or newspapers or what appear to be coffee-stained manuscripts. I sit carefully on the edge of a chair that looks ancient. The spindly legs wobble, but hold.

M. Aubier leans forward and stretches forward a hand. It is dusty with age spots. Bones move visibly beneath the blemished skin. His hand touches my knee. With every visit there is the touching. Every visit. It is as though M. Aubier wants to assure himself that I am real. Or that he is still alive.

"Some tea, M. Schiller? I just fixed myself a cup a few moments ago."

"No, no, Marie, Herr Schiller needs something stronger than your chamomile tea. Bring me the wine bottle. Yes, yes, the red. Red is best for cutting the dust. My throat always gets so dry when I travel. It is as though it were coated with dust."

I only smile and nod. When one is around M. Aubier one does not have to speak often. That is one of the reasons I enjoy visiting his apartment. Certainly, I am a man of words, but I prefer to write mine down.

As Marie Aubier gathers up the wine I close my eyes. M. is correct. It has been a long day and I am tired. The train was noisy and hot and full of people with restless eyes. This summer has been decorated with people of restless eyes. All the talk of tension between nations has put the wind up in them. Saber rattling scares the average man. For months I have been afraid. Not since Christmas have I had a really sound night's sleep. Uncle Franz, my father's brother, is in the government. Minister of some minor function. At one time he was involved with the railroads, but during the winter changes were made. Uncle Franz says the Kaiser will not be trifled with. According to my uncle, Wilhelm is volatile. Once, Franz called him a Prussian volcano. I wrote a poem about that. I have never submitted it for publication.

The scents of soap and vanilla drift to my nostrils and I open my eyes. Madame Aubier is standing before me smiling. She has taken a moment to dab a drop of vanilla extract behind each ear and her face shines. Without speaking she offers me a goblet of wine. The goblet is crystal, finely etched. She hands her husband a goblet. It is crystal, too, but the goblets do not match.

M. Aubier raises his glass and clears his throat. He has a marvelous voice, deep, resonant, mellow. Often I have wondered why he never took up the stage or politics. After all, they are much in the same.

"A toast, Herr Schiller, a toast to our continued success."

"To success," I echo.

"And to peace," Madame chimes in.

"Of course, my dear." Monsieur leans closer and whispers conspiratorially, "Madame is quite nervous this summer. She is convinced that 1914 will be different than every other year." He laughs and we sip at our wine.

"But the newspapers," she says, her hands tremble faintly as fingers point at the papers. Looking around, I can see that newspapers are piled on the floor and on several chairs. Editions are all mixed up. Even a quick glance reveals that several feature prominent articles on the escalating tensions in the Balkans. Headlines reference Serbia and Austria. Such names mean little to me for I read more poems and novels than newspapers. Such behavior may no longer be wise. My uncle would tell me to remain informed. If I were bolder I would tell him I am well informed, on more important matters.

"All they talk of is war." Madame picks up three newspapers at random. One of them has today's date. "War is coming, There May Be War, Can War Be Avoided?"

"Yes, yes, I'll admit it sounds glum, Marie. But you must remember, every summer there is talk of war. One year it was Turkey. Another summer, Greece. This year the eye of the world is on Serbia." Monsieur shakes his head. "A curious place. I visited there once. 1903, I think." He sips his wine. "Have you been to Serbia, Herr Schiller?"

"No, I have not had the pleasure," I say. Frankly, I have little desire to travel anywhere and no interest whatsoever in going to Serbia. I would far prefer to stay in my room and write. However, Monsieur Aubier is my publisher. Politics are important in the publishing world, too. "I was however, in Austria, in April."

"Ah, Austria, what beautiful snows they have there," exclaims Madame and the conversation is off. I can safely sip my wine, nod my head, and murmur "oh really" now and then. The Aubiers love to talk, most especially when they have an appreciative audience. I am a good listener.

I sip my wine and the let their chatter flow over me like

a pleasant breeze. It is not a particularly cool one, but pleasant nonetheless. For weeks the air has been hot and still and even the thought of the word breeze makes me smile.

After a few minutes the conversation falters and we all sit in companionable silence, reluctant to move on to the tasks at hand. There are contracts to be discussed and books to be autographed. A pile of them in one corner leans casually against the wall. But there seems no hurry. Nothing monumental ever seems to happen: days spin on and on, some hot, some cold, children are born and old men die, yet nothing much happens. All of which is fine with me. I am partial to the subtle, the properly placed comma, the color of a ripe persimmon, the unique brush strokes of a master.

The room grows quiet. So faintly that it seems more a dream than reality, the notes of the violin drift into the room. The girl plays well today.

A cart rumbles by outside the window. The horse's hooves ring out against the pavement.

Madame's stomach rumbles and she blushes. She looks younger when she blushes.

A flicker of movement catches my eye. I wait and then it comes again, just at the edge of vision. Only when it occurs for the third time do I recognize it.

The curtains at the window are fluttering. At first they move only sporadically, briefly. But in a few minutes they are dancing in a breeze that has risen from the hot earth. I glance at M. Aubier. He is looking at me. We hold each other's glance for a moment. Then he makes caterpillar movements with his massive eyebrows.

I rise and wander to the window. Across Rue Rampart the flags on the Plaza de Enfants are flapping in the rising wind. Papers blow down the sidewalk. A man loses his hat and goes chasing after it. People turn and stare at the sky.

Off to the west clouds are beginning to mass. Purple rims these clouds and I wonder.

A new sound floats down the street. Around the corner a band has begun to play. The tune is vaguely familiar. After a moment I place it. It is a martial tune. Our local regiment plays it on parade days.

"What is going on?" M. Aubier is curious. I can hear the curiosity running through his voice, coloring it. He is a curious man, and that curiosity has served him well over the years in his business. A curious publisher finds the new talent.

"Looks like a parade," I say. Flags are waving from windows across the way and I can no longer hear the blue violin.

"There are marching," says M. Aubier, "but why?"

"War," cries Madame, "the war must have come."

"Oh, don't be silly," M. says. Every summer governments talk of war and every summer passes into autumn and nothing has happened. It is commerce, see. Commerce has tied all of Europe together like threads in a tapestry. These days, businessmen run every country. They don't want war, see. War disrupts trade and they certainly do not want their livelihoods inconvenienced."

"Oh, Pierre, I do not know. People are not like they were when we were young. No, no, they are not. Oh, I don't know."

I do not know either. M. Aubier is certainly a successful man of business, but this summer has been a strange one and, to me, the atmosphere seems foreboding. But then I am poet and often overly sensitive. The band has passed by now and the street is empty. Across the plaza the little boy is still standing with the old grandmother. But he has lost his balloon. I feel my line of sight drift up, up, up, until suddenly I see the balloon. The red balloon. It looks like a pinprick of blood on a great blue sea.

KSU Entrance

my leige

Mark Kinnaird

don't think I've forgotten you
how you smelled
the way you liked to live
a little closer to the edge
than any woman I've ever met
I can't forget
how you would run your finger
across the back of my neck
until I couldn't stand it anymore
or how you kissed like no one ever has
so subtle just a brush against my lips
giving me enough but still wanting a little more
I can't forget how we made love under the stars
the milky way witness to all our stories
our swearing some kind of allegiance
to be there for one another
through trials and tribulations
don't think I've forgotten
that my time and place were laid asunder
and how easy it was for you to forget me

muskogee 1982

Mark Kinnaird

left kentucky at midnight and drove
all night long just to run away from home
and i drove with an abandon
reckless and barely noticing what passed my window
streaking through west
memphis where those boys
were killed by some guy
who had nothing better to do
and finally "oklahoma is ok"
I believed it because I needed to
I missed the azalea festival in muskogee
I had no idea what an azalea looked like
but some waitress told me
as we sipped beer on the edge of the dance floor
I still remember how my hands felt on her hips
I still wonder what she saw in me when I saw not much
when I kissed her I felt like I had grown up all at once
honky tonk music fell at our feet
as we tried to understand
where we were going with our lives
we needed to not make a dent in each other
to touch and part with just memories
I know she must look on me like a snapshot
of a time when her life was simpler
and that was all we ever wanted

A Complete Departure

Linda McAuliffe

A Novel Excerpt

I saw the worry on my sister Ella's face. And Nancy's. I'd just scared them both with another one of my respiratory episodes. Oh, don't get me wrong, it was frightening for me, too. That feeling of struggling for air to breathe is about as chilling as it gets. But after all I've been through, there's nothing that unmoors me, at least not yet.

I watched them as best as I could although I can't control my eyes. If I could, I'd have been able to give my sister and myself what we both desperately needed, a way for me to communicate with her. A yes/no response, that's all we've ever wanted, but even that wasn't meant to be.

I'm paralyzed from the neck down, I can't breathe on my own, I can't shit on my own. People take care of all those things for me. I know that a lot of people with traumatic brain and spinal cord injuries can talk, but not me. I watch documentaries and YouTube videos about people with those types of injuries so I know what people can do. I even watched a documentary about assisted suicide. Not that that is an option for me, since I can't communicate. To be honest, I'm surprised Ella permitted me to watch it. Often, she just seems to know what I want to watch, what I'd be interested in.

Oh, I was bitter for a long time; but after a few years of that, of wishing that I could just die, I came to a certain level of acceptance of my life and of my condition. What keeps me going is Ella. I know it would be devastating for her to lose me.

It all happened nearly ten years ago. I can remember it well. I remember my past life better than I remember yesterday, which may be a blessing for me. Retreating to past memories helps me pass the time. Thank goodness for Nancy, my full-time caregiver, and Ella. They keep me entertained. At least my mind. I have people in addition to them who move my body, keep me turned, get me in my chair so my body moves.

It was the Friday after Thanksgiving. My buddies from high school were in town for the holiday so we decided to play PS4 at Ken's house in Bald Knob, like we used to when we went to Franklin County High School. David was driving, so Larry, Ken, and I could drink. We stayed late into the night, at least 1:00 or so. An icy rain fell as we made our way down the gravel driveway in the car, a Toyota Camry. Larry rode up front while I stretched out in the back seat, feeling the five beers I drank. I was asleep in no time.

That's the last thing I remember until I woke up in the hospital five days later. I couldn't move a muscle, couldn't even open my eyes. The first thing I remember is the antiseptic smells all around me. I didn't feel my body, which gave me false comfort. I remember thinking I couldn't be hurt that bad if I couldn't feel pain. My mind wouldn't let me process what that really meant.

Sometime later, I'm not sure how long since time was fuzzy, I could open my eyes. The first face I saw was my father's. I heard the nurse comment about him not leaving my side. I didn't see Mom until later that evening, which didn't surprise me, Mom was not really the hospital type. Ella was there soon after I woke up. She told me Keith, our younger brother, had been there but had to return to his job in Tennessee.

Ella was the one who told me what's what, with my father holding one hand and her holding the other. She laid it all out for me. Since I'd been lying down in the back seat, the vertebrae in my neck were crushed. The car hit a tree and I was thrown into the door of the car, the momentum from my body damaging my neck. I was lucky to be alive. She told me about the paralysis and the unlikelihood that I would ever get movement back. I would be on a ventilator for the rest of my life. I tried to focus on her face but my eyes darted around the room, just like they do now.

She tried not to, but she cried as she got the last of it out, and she was the one who wiped the tears that fell from my eyes. I'm always grateful for those tears I shed. I think that is what convinced her that I understood her, that my mind was alive and well in a broken and shattered body. The hardest person for me to look at was Dad, the look on his face tore me apart. I saw the defeat in his eyes, the realization that he could do nothing for me, that he couldn't fix this.

Then there was mother. She came into the room, dressed to the nines. She must have gone home to dress up.

When she saw I was awake she draped herself over me and cried, "My baby boy, my baby boy." Damn, she was acting as if I was dead! Dad pulled her off and tried to get her out of the room. I figured she knew I was paralyzed. They had all known for days now, before I woke up.

"We'll have to find a home for my baby," Mom said.

Dad shushed her. Ella was more direct. "Stop it, Mom. He's not going to a nursing home."

"I didn't say a nursing home. There must be nice places for people like him. Only the best for my baby." There it was again. Now I was her baby, though she wanted to put me away. I couldn't imagine life in a nursing home. I was twenty-six years old, for God's sake.

Dad spoke up. "He'll be here in the hospital for a while, so we've got time to figure things out, but I want him home with us, hon."

I couldn't see her but I could imagine the horrified look on her face. I did hear her gasp.

"I'll help Mom, Dad," said Ella. No surprise there.

I was in the hospital for three weeks until they determined that I didn't need around-the-clock medical care. Ella and Dad saved my life during that time, they never stopped talking to me, never stopped reassuring me that they would take care of me. I saw Mom less and less during that period. I did hear her from the hallway the night that Dad put his foot down about me coming home while Mom still pushed to put me away into a "home," as she put it. I remember her prophetic words. "I can't do this."

Dad and Ella arranged all the details, I heard them talking. And they always kept me informed. They would transform my old room, which happened to be one of the largest bedrooms in the house, into a repository for a hospital bed and all the medical equipment I would need. Years ago, Dad and Mom had been able to buy a larger house as Dad moved up at the grocery store and Mom began working at the local utilities company. Mom had given me the best room and Ella the smallest, because, frankly, she liked me better.

Mom was absent for all this planning, for one reason or another. She went back to work as soon as I was out of the woods while Dad took Family and Medical Leave to stay with me. My Mom and Dad had the kind of relationship where Mom cried and cajoled and Dad gave in to keep the peace. Mom wanted me in a nursing home, working to convince everyone that they couldn't care for me at home when the truth was she didn't want to care for me. Having someone dependent on her, even her precious first-born son, was more than she could handle, more than she bargained for.

Despite her adamancy, Dad was unmoved. He would have me at home and he would care for me, even if Mom wouldn't. I struggled with his decision even then. The last thing I wanted to be was a burden on my family but I didn't want to live in a nursing home. The day I moved back home was the start of my new life, and I hoped that we could all handle it.

Third

(The Long Night)

P. F. Powers

What was the coroner thinking?
Another one bites the dust?
1:15 a.m. call. Coffee? Toast? No, too early.
But death is so final.
No need to rush.

The beloved white couch replaced by a hospital bed
Ceramic ballerina, releve frozen in time
On the small dresser beside the door
Cat litter box in the closet
Pink and purple flowered quilt covering her.

The only window draws me to it.
Waiting for headlights to appear through the blackness
I see two faint eyes in the distance.
Don't come any closer, I'm not ready.
But your arrival is inevitable.

Who will greet me this time? I never know.
Will it be the insanity of grief or the calmness of denial?
Tonight, calm.
Calmness encased so tightly, release will be staggering.
But not yet. Not at this moment in time.

I slowly wheel her from this house
Unaware she is leaving a home she loved
With its hot tub, pool, two old gray cats, and a man she
adored.
I will never know she also left behind
A demented mother having just lost her third.

Switzer Bridge

M Raine (signature)

My Love of Reading

Melissa Ann Raine

I have loved reading books since I was one year old. There is a picture of me sitting cross-legged in the round lid of a wicker basket. In the picture I was staring at the pages of a board-book clutched in my chubby hands as if it held the secrets of the universe.

And maybe at the time it did.

But once I got older, I wanted to read more books or, if the words were too hard for me to read on my own, listen to more stories. When I was three or four, I was introduced to a building that held all the secrets of the universe. And these secrets were held in tons of books sitting on the shelves. And the people called librarians, who read stories to children like me during 'story-time,' were the keepers of these secrets.

The building that held the secrets is now known as the Old Paul Sawyier Public Library. The current Paul Sawyier Public Library sits next door to it. But when I was a kid, the old building was called *The* Paul Sawyier Library.

It is a large, striking building that towers three stories, almost the same height as the Good Shepherd School that sits across the street. It was housed between an equally grand, iron sculpture called the Singing Bridge and a drab parking lot. The parking lot is gone now but the Old Library building still stands in the same place today.

For me, it was a building from another time, built out of white stone slabs that glowed in the sunlight. The front steps are black-and-white marble, the dark spots are arranged in appealing asymmetrical flecks, like the spots on a Dalmatian. When the sunlight hits them just right they sparkle.

Every time I climbed those four steps with my mom and entered through the double glass doors, I knew I was entering a palace of books. Everything about the library was magical. I was enchanted by the idea of being allowed to borrow as many books as I could carry and take them home without having to pay for them. When I was finished reading the books, I could return them and get more.

The smell of the first floor would hit me as soon as I walked up to the front desk to drop off my latest collection of books. It was a mixture of the musky vanilla scent that wafted from the aging pages of the books that rested on the shelves and a deep, almost oaky scent. I never could pin down the source of that smell and, as wonderful as the new Paul Sawyier Public Library is, it is this scent of old history that I miss whenever I walk in to check out books.

My family and I spent very little time on the first floor. After we returned our borrowed books, we would walk up the curving staircase. The steps were the same patterned marble as the front steps. As soon as we got to the second-floor landing, we would pass through another set of glass doors and enter the children's section. This was where the children's and teen books were kept. The room held the same scent as the first floor — books aging on the shelf like bottles of vintage wine. But it was mixed with sweeter smells: the yeasty smell of fresh Play-Doh, baby powder, and the nose-tingling scent of plastic warming in the sun.

I would either go into the smaller room where the story-time programs took place or Mom would let me browse through the stacks. The stacks I remember making a bee-line to were in the non-fiction section.

My first love was learning about animals and their habitats. I had no time to read about fairies and unicorns. I didn't see why I should read about something that did not exist. Learning about the real world was magical enough for me. Some of the first books I checked out of the library were small picture books about nature, the human body, and animals.

I had a phase in second grade where I read everything about the five senses — touch, taste, sight, sound, and smell — that I could get my hands on. This is when I first became aware — for only a brief few seconds in kid-time — that when I get interested in something, I immerse myself in it. I wallow in all the knowledge of this subject until the next interest comes along.

I never outgrew this thirst for knowledge or my tendency to get wrapped up in a particular subject. But thanks to being able to borrow books from the library, I could read as many as I wanted. Money was never an issue. Unless I turned in a book late. There was a late fee, but I did my best to keep an eye on my library books so I didn't have to pay late fees often.

I love reading books because the words are on the page right in front of me. Unlike when I'm listening to a teacher or someone telling me new information, I don't have to ask the book to repeat itself. I also don't have to worry that it will get impatient with me if I don't understand what I'm reading or if I ask it too many questions. Living with an auditory processing learning disability has left me with lingering self-doubt about my ability to understand what I hear.

I've come so far from when I was first diagnosed around five years old. I've been able to work around the disability, but I still second-guess myself. I wonder, even if it is just for a second, if I understood what someone told me. Then I wonder, even when I'm correct, if the person who I was talking to is secretly mad at me for being so slow to understand what they said.

With a book, the words are on each white page available for repeated readings. The book feels not impatience and doesn't judge who is reading it. Best of all, the sentences are always in the same order they were printed in. Nothing gets rearranged or lost with repeated readings, as sometimes happens when a story is told out loud over and over again.

My love of reading has expanded my horizons beyond Frankfort as well as helping me learn more about Frankfort. I love reading not only because I get to learn all the secrets of the universe, but because reading lets me go on many adventures. I get to make friends, fall in love, and fight evil without having to leave my comfort zone.

At the same time, my inner adventures gave me the courage, one book at a time, to eventually leave my comfort zone and interact with the world around me.

When the outside world gets too rough, reading is my bolt-hole. A secret place where I can rest and gain strength until I'm ready to face the world again.

Books are my talismans and teachers.

I can't imagine life without books. And I hope I never have to go without them.

Singing Bridge

The Path

Mary Helen Weeks

Your path calls your name
   Your Heritage
Your path knows your name
Slow up, Be Present
Release my beauty

I found a feather
   You are following your path
You don't give up
   how you were made
You don't give up
   your Soul
I offer the most beautiful
   Of what I am

Out to Pasture

Virginia Smith

A Novel Excerpt

From Chapter 1

… Forty minutes later, Becky turned from a two-lane country road onto the paved driveway of the old converted farmhouse where she worked. She noted with satisfaction the freshly painted letters on the wooden sign in the front yard: Out to Pasture, A Thoroughbred Retirement Farm. That faded sign had bugged her for the two months since she came to work here, and she finally took matters into her own hands and repainted it a few days ago. It looked much better. Nice, even. At the rear of the house she parked beside the boss's pickup, in front of the small barn where they stored supplies for their fifteen retired Thoroughbred champions.

She got out of the car and leaned against the open door to let her gaze sweep over the deep green Kentucky horse farm. Double rows of black plank fencing divided gently rolling swells of pasture. Heavy dew clung to the grass, sparkling in the sunlight on this crisp spring morning. She turned and looked across the road, where the mares with their foals were pastured. The babies hung close to their mothers today. Sometimes they ran and frolicked, and Becky loved to watch their graceful movements as they stretched their limbs and tested their limits. They seemed to know they were a special breed among horses. Thoroughbreds. Born to run, to train as elite equine athletes, and perhaps even to win that coveted Kentucky prize—a blanket of roses.

Becky leaned into the car and snatched the bag of carrots from the passenger seat. A muted bark reached her ears, and she glanced toward the back door of the farmhouse that served as the retirement farm's office and founder Neal Haldeman's home. The wooden door stood open, indicating the boss was already out and about, as usual. But Neal's yellow Labrador retriever stood on hind legs inside the house, his front paws pressed against the glass storm door, barking. Odd. Neal always let Sam out first thing in the morning. Why was the dog still inside? Becky scanned the paddocks but saw no sign of her boss. He must be in the barn. She slammed the car door and headed toward the house.

Galloping hooves thundered behind her, accompanied by a loud whinny. She turned to see Alidor racing across the turf toward her. Her pulse picked up speed, pounding in rhythm with the sound of his hooves. He arrived at the black plank fence, turned sideways, and came to a quick stop.

Alidor frightened her. He was the biggest of the champions at the Pasture, and the meanest. No stallion was nice, according to Neal, but Alidor's fiery personality and aggressive behavior had scared even him when the horse first arrived. Becky stayed as far away from Alidor as she could, and he ignored her completely.

But not this morning. Alidor continued to whinny, his ears pinned almost flat to his head, his lips pulled back to show his teeth and gums. She had never heard that loud, high-pitched sound from any of the horses. Her stomach tightened at the urgency in the stallion's tone.

Surely Neal would hear and come to investigate. She glanced at the barn. Seeing no movement, she took a hesitant step toward the agitated horse.

"What's wrong, Alidor?"

Alidor tossed his head and pawed the ground with a front hoof. Becky took a few more steps. Maybe he smelled the carrots. Should she offer him one? Her heart thudded with fear. He had been known to bite and was one of the stallions Neal would not let visitors feed.

Besides, he didn't look hungry or as if he was demanding a treat. He looked distressed.

Swallowing against a dry throat, Becky drew closer to the disturbed animal. She kept her voice low, the way Neal did when he talked to the stallions.

"It's okay, Alidor. Whatever it is, I'll find Neal and he'll take care of it."

As she neared the fence, she could see the rear of the barn. The back door stood open.

"Neal?" she called in that direction. "Something's wrong with Alidor. Are you in there?"

Nothing.

In the next paddock, Rusty Racer ran to the nearest corner and took up Alidor's cry. And behind Alidor's paddock,

Founder's Fortune also began to call out in a loud whinny. Ten feet in front of her Alidor tossed his head repeatedly, white showing all around the intense dark depths of his eye.

The skin on her neck prickled at the sound in stereo. She'd only worked at the Pasture for two months, and she had never seen the horses act this way. Whatever was wrong with Alidor was getting to the others as well, and she didn't have a clue what to do. Where was Neal?

"Neal!" Her voice, sharp with worry, sliced through the cool morning air like a blade.

His cell phone. Yes, that's what she'd do, she'd call his cell phone. She ran toward the barn. That extension was closer than the phone in the office. Alidor trotted along the fence, keeping pace with her, whinnying as he ran.

Rounding the corner, she shot through the open barn door. Inside, she tripped over something and landed face down on the dirt floor with a hard thud. The bag of carrots flew out of her hand.

"What in the world?" She rolled over to see what had tripped her. And screamed.

Neal lay in the dust, a pool of dark liquid beneath his head. Outside the barn, Alidor and the other horses fell silent.

time of your life

Mark Kinnaird

under the night sky
as the heavens lighten
the stars slowly disappear
amongst the branches
and the fall leaves
you know the chill of night
will burn off
the birds will begin their songs
feeling your world come to life
and elections
and wars
and rumors of wars
don't exist for a while
it is that fleeting moment
when you can believe
there is something
right about the world

Remember This

Ginny Patrick

"C'mon, Jen. Try to remember. Think of our table at Maguire's. The funny waiter with the hairpiece that makes us laugh."

The man standing in front of her — Patrick, he said his name was — peered at her through eyes that held enough hurt to stir guilt in the pit of her stomach. She ought to remember him. She wanted to! But where the memories should be inside her aching head lay nothing but a fuzzy gray mist.

Perched on the edge of the hospital bed, Jennifer clenched the sterile white sheets and swallowed against a medicinally dry mouth. A waiter with a hairpiece? Maybe if she focused...

"I think — "

Hope surged into his features, and he took an eager step toward her. "Yes?"

The elusive image receded into the mist. She shook her head, tears burning her eyes. "I can't."

Patrick's shoulders slumped, disappointment etched in

33

the lines on either side of his mouth. "It's okay, sweetheart. The doctor says your memory will return eventually. In the meantime, let's focus on our blessings. You're lucky to be alive after that car wreck. The Toyota is a total loss."

Jennifer half-heard his words, but her attention was drawn to the lips that spoke them. Generous lips that tightened with pain but softened to speak words of comfort. Something about his lips sent the fog in her brain swirling enough to glimpse a shadowy memory. She rose from the hospital bed and wavered in a sudden wave of dizziness.

Patrick rushed forward to support her. "Maybe you shouldn't try to stand. You've been in bed for a week."

She raised her hand and brushed a fingertip across his mouth. "Would you kiss me? I—I think it might help."

Doubt and longing battled in the dark eyes that searched her face, but he hesitated only a moment. His head descended toward hers, and she tilted her face to meet his kiss. Tentative at first, barely a brush of soft skin against her mouth. She inhaled the scent of him, a fragrant blend of cologne and soap, and the cloud in her brain churned.

A word surfaced. Eternity. She'd given him a bottle of the expensive cologne for Christmas.

Encouraged, she pressed into the kiss. Memories surged. Hanging pictures in their apartment, and Patrick's kiss when they stood back to admire their work. The candlelight dinner she burned on their first anniversary and his kiss before he picked up the phone to order pizza. The agony of yet another negative pregnancy test, which even his kisses couldn't soothe.

"Albert," she whispered against his lips.

He pulled back, alarm coloring his face. "Sweetheart, I'm Patrick."

She smiled. "The waiter with the hairpiece. His name is Albert. I remember."

She wrapped her arms around his neck and pulled him back into their kiss.

Old State Capitol

melancholy

Mark Kinnaird

all that i write is tinted
with the blues and hues of colors
that exists only in my imagination
i long for your kiss
and you're telling me that all is ok
so i can understand
why some things can never be
and it has been
so long
since so longs were simple
uttered words
and not an epitaph
that never let me dance
and never let me call out to you and
knowing you would have been a joy
i put your picture amidst your brother
and sister right in the middle
where you were and catching up is
contagious among the living
and i imagine that you are the one
who learned to dance
among the dew sodden grasses
at earliest light
when the sky's colors

are only possible in paintings
and the touch of light feet
skipping across the earth are your first steps
and i demand to be let go and
dance with you but i never find the key
to open my own heart
so i never expect others to do the same
because im afraid that you mistook me for
an empty spot on the horizon where the sun once
 was but now nightfall comes
and cleans the tragedies away
and we can all look at the milky way
and wonder how to talk and dance
and finally laugh

Rural Well

The Neighbor's Lament

Michael Embry

Tom put on the ear protectors and turned the ignition on the riding lawnmower. The red machine roared to life inside the work shed. He put it into reverse gear and slowly backed out of the building. He then turned the steering wheel, pressed down on the accelerator and started up the side of the lawn as grass shot out of the side.

The sun was out but it was still cool in the early morning air. Tom was the early bird in the neighborhood, preferring to do yard work before it got too hot. He also liked to get a head start on Fred, his next door neighbor on the right side, in getting his yard mowed and trimmed. Mrs. Barrett, who lived on the other side, was an aging widow who paid to have her yard mowed every week or so, whether it needed it or not.

Tom glanced over at Fred's house several times. He hadn't seen Fred, his wife Joan, or their three kids in several days. He wasn't really complaining, especially with the children not being around since they created enough commotion for several families.

After finishing the lawn, Tom sat on the front porch with a tall glass of tea. The air was getting warmer. He was pleased to have finished that chore, and gained some satisfaction when he heard some other lawnmowers down the street. He wondered if Fred would be out soon to mow his lawn. It really looked tall and ragged next to his manicured yard.

A few minutes later the mailman walked up to the porch and handed Tom several magazines and envelopes.

"Morning," Tom said. "Beautiful day."

"I agree," the mailman said, then looked over at Fred's house. "Have you seen the Bergmans lately?"

Tom shrugged. "Not in several days."

"I've got a stash of mail for them. Their mailbox is packed now. They didn't leave a stop mail notice or anything at the post office. I thought they might be on vacation or away for some reason."

"Not that I know of," Tom said. "Want me to take their mail?"

"No, that's okay. I'll just hold it until I hear from them." The mailman smiled and headed to Mrs. Barrett's house. "Have a nice day."

"Same to you."

Tom looked over at Fred's house. Nothing really looked peculiar, other than a lawn that needed to be mowed. He sat back down on the rocker and finished his tea.

"Anything the matter?" His wife, Alice, stood at the door. "You looked like you were lost in your thoughts."

"Oh, just relaxing," Tom said. "Huh, by the way, have

you seen Fred or Joan lately?"

"No. Why do you ask?"

"The mailman said he has a stack of mail for them and was wondering if we had heard anything."

"It's been several days," she said. "Do you think we should check or give the police a call?"

"Nah," Tom said with a shrug. "They probably made a short trip and didn't want anyone to know. I bet they'll return today or tomorrow."

"You're probably right," Alice said. "Can I get you some more tea?

"No thanks. I'll be in in a few minutes to take a shower and get cleaned up. Still want to see a movie this afternoon?"

"Yep. There's a two o'clock showing of that new Leonardo DiCaprio movie, so we have time to get ready."

Alice went back into the house. A few minutes later Tom stood and walked to the front door. He looked over at Fred's place for a few seconds before opening the door and stepping inside.

After showering and eating lunch, Tom turned on the television and flipped channels while Alice was getting dressed. Nothing interested him so he turned it off.

"I'll be ready in five minutes," Alice said from the bathroom.

"Take your time." Tom went to the kitchen and sorted through the mail. Most of it was junk and it was tossed in the trashcan. There were two magazines, and he picked up one turned a few pages before Alice came in, wrapping a sweater around her shoulders.

"Let's go," Tom said with a smile.

Pulling out of the driveway, Tom eased the car into the

Michael Embry

quiet neighborhood street. Alice looked at the Bergman's house as they drove by.

"It doesn't look like anybody's home," she said.

"I bet they took off for a long weekend," Tom said.

"Probably."

After the movie, they stopped at a couple stores before going home. When they got inside Alice noticed the red-blinking light on the telephone, notifying them they had missed a call.

"Probably a salesperson," Tom said. "I'm not expecting any calls." They left the phone blinking.

He picked up the magazines and they went to the den. They perused the magazines and didn't turn on the TV.

"I could take a nap," Tom said after a yawn. "Either that, or I'm going to drop off here in the recliner."

"If you're hungry I'll order pizza," Alice said.

"Sounds good. Wake me up when it arrives."

After ordering the pizza, Alice dialed the message number. She punched in another number to listen again.

"Come here, Tom," she said, raising her voice.

"What is it?" he said, getting out of the recliner.

"That phone message was from Val Bergman. She's concerned about her family."

"What do you mean?"

"She left a message and said that she'd been trying to reach her family since this morning but no one has answered."

"Like I said, they probably went on a short trip. They probably didn't think to tell Valerie."

"I'm worried. Why don't you go over to their house?"

"Well, give me a few minutes," Tom said. "I need to put on my shoes."

A few minutes later, the doorbell rang. The pizza was delivered. Alice paid for the pizza and sat it down on the kitchen table.

"Mind if I eat before it gets cold?" Tom said.

Alice shook her head in a disapproving manner. Tom didn't seem to notice and took a slice from the box.

"Please, Tom," she said.

"Oh, okay." He took the slice with him as he left the house.

Tom rang the doorbell several times and then knocked on the front door when there wasn't a response. He turned to return home when he noticed Alice on the front porch.

"Tom, go around back and see if anything looks suspicious."

Tom shook his head and rolled his eyes. "Okay, if it'll make you happy."

He slowly walked around to the rear of the house, then knocked on the back door. He peeked inside the kitchen window. Some food, coffee cups, cereal bowls and an open newspaper were scattered on the counter.

On the way back, he glanced in the garage. Their red SUV was parked inside. Tom thought that was odd since that was the vehicle they used most of the time. He turned around and noticed their small pickup.

"Did you see anything?" Alice asked when he returned home.

Tom had a perplexed look on his face. "Well, their vehicles are still there and the kitchen was kinda messy."

"Do you think we should call the police?"

"I don't know," Tom said, shrugging his shoulders before picking up a cold slice of pizza. "I'd hate to do something rash if they've only been gone a little while on an errand."

"But what if something's the matter?"

"Honey, let's give it a few more hours. Why don't you call Valerie and tell her we checked on the house. I don't think anything's wrong."

"If you say so," she said with a look of concern.

Tom went to the den and turned on the TV. He sat back in his recliner, and within ten minutes, he had dozed off to sleep. Alice went outside with a magazine and sat on the porch swing. She wasn't out there for fifteen minutes when the phone rang. She knew Tom wouldn't answer it so she got up and hurried to answer it.

"I was wondering if you've heard anything from my parents?" Valerie asked. "I've called everywhere I thought they could be. I only get the answering machine when I call mom and dad's cell phones. I'm really worried."

"We haven't heard or seen a thing," Alice said, trying to keep her voice calm. "I'm sure they've gone for a short trip and you'll hear from them soon."

"Would you mind going back over there and look in the windows?"

"I'll do that right now."

"Please call me right back when you get back."

Alice went to the doorway to the den and heard Tom snoring. She decided not to disturb him and go to the Bergman's house by herself. It was still daylight although the sun beginning to fade, casting long shadows from the pine trees that separated their property.

She knocked on the front door and rang the doorbell, even though she wasn't expecting anyone to answer. She waited a few seconds, then peeked in the picture window to the living room. All was quiet and still. She turned to go to the side window when she was startled by a figure standing several feet behind her.

"Is something the matter, ma'am? Locked out of your house?"

Alice clutched her chest and took a deep breath. "Officer, you scared me. I didn't hear you come up behind me."

"Sorry about that, ma'am," he said with a soft smile.

"We haven't heard from our neighbors and their daughter asked me to come over and see if they were here. My husband checked this morning. We think they might have gone on a short trip."

"What's their name?"

"Bergman."

Alice followed the officer as he went to the side of the house. He glanced inside a bedroom window for a few seconds, then banged on it for a few seconds with an open hand.

"What's the matter?" Joan asked.

"There appears to be someone in the bed."

The officer took a phone from his belt and dialed 911. He gave the dispatcher details on what he'd seen and said to send an ambulance and police. He went back to the front door but was unable to open it.

The officer ran to the back door and turned the knob, then took a flashlight from his belt and broke a panel glass. He reached in and turned the deadbolt lock and opened the door. A minute later, an emergency medical vehicle and two police cars pulled in front of the house.

Alice was standing on the front porch when the officer opened the front door.

"Bodies in the front and back bedrooms," the officer

told the paramedics. "I believe they're dead."

The other police officers followed the paramedics into the house. "You better stay here," the officer told Alice. It didn't take long before several neighbors came out of their houses and began heading toward the Bergman's home.

Several windows in the house were opened. The officer came outside, and drooped with his hands to his knees. Alice bent down next to him.

"Are you okay?" she asked.

"Carbon monoxide," he said.

"What?"

"The house was filled with carbon monoxide." He coughed and stood. "They died from carbon-monoxide poisoning."

"Oh, my god. How do you know?"

"The techs have a gauge. That's why we're airing the house out."

Another EMS vehicle parked in front of the house. The techs carried two gurneys into the house, and, within minutes, two covered bodies were carried out of the house.

"What's going on?"

Alice turned around and Tom was approaching from the side.

"They all died from carbon monoxide," Alice said before letting loose a burst of tears and rushing to his open arms.

Tom held her tightly as they watched two more bodies being taken to the EMT vehicle.

"Do you know any next of kin?" an officer asked them.

"They have a daughter," Tom said. "We can give you her number."

"I'd appreciate that."

Alice went to the house while Tom stepped closer to the front door. He could see someone moving about inside.

"Any idea how this happened?" Tom asked the officer next to him.

"No clue. We'll have someone from the state fire marshal's office here to check things out in the house."

"Could it be a suicide?"

"We don't know," the officer said. "That's only speculation at this point." He glanced at the door. "I need to go back inside."

Alice returned with Valerie's phone number on a piece of paper and handed it to Tom.

"Do you think we should go ahead and call her?" Alice asked.

"I think so. Just tell her that it's an emergency and she needs to get here."

Tom waited for the officer to return while Alice walked to the side of the yard to call Val. Tom glanced over and noticed Alice wiping tears from her face. The officer came out of the house and Tom gave him Val's phone number.

The EMT vehicles left at the same time, their red lights flashing but sirens mute. Several neighbors walked over to Tom and he told them what had happened. Children were across the street playing tag, apparently oblivious of what happened.

Alice returned with tears in her eyes.

"Are you okay?" Tom asked.

"It was awful talking to her." She took a tissue from her pocket and wiped her eyes. "I told her we'd pick her up at the airport. She's going to call me and give me details a little later."

"Let's go home," Tom said, placing his arm around her

shoulders and giving her a gentle squeeze. Her head rested against his chest as they ambled back to the house. The neighbors also began walking slowly to their houses.

Tom sat down at the kitchen table. Alice went to the re-frigerator and took out two cans of cola and sat down with him. He took a big swallow and lowered his head. Joan reached over and rested her hand on his forearm.

"This is so unreal," he said. "To see someone the night before, and then the next day they're dead. I just don't un-derstand how it could happen."

"I know what you mean," she said.

"The officer told me that there should be a preliminary finding after the fire marshal investigates and the coroner's office performs the autopsies. He said we may know some-thing in the morning."

"I feel so sorry for Valerie," Alice said. "I just can't im-agine how she must feel right now."

"I'm sure totally helpless."

Tom went to the den and sat in the recliner. Before long, he was snoring. He was awakened with Alice tapping him on the shoulder.

"Val just called. She's already at the airport."

"Our airport— Blue Grass?"

Tom quickly got up and they were out of the house within five minutes. The airport was about 30 minutes away. About halfway there Alice received another call from Val, telling her that she'd be waiting outside the front lobby."

When they arrived, Val picked up her travel bag and approached the car. Alice got out and hugged her. A car came up behind them and honked. Alice and Val seemed oblivious to the sound, but a couple more beeps, and they got inside.

Val sat in the backseat and listened as Tom and Alice explained what apparently had happened. Val occasionally sniffled and wiped away tears as they made their way back to the neighborhood.

When they arrived a yellow tape crossed the front entrance. The door and several windows were still open. At the bottom of the driveway was a red fire marshal's SUV.

Tom walked to the front door and knocked several times. A few seconds later a man in a uniform holding a meter stepped outside. He quietly told him who they were and the fire officer walked over to Val.

Val wept as she listened to the officer explain what they believe happened to her family. When it was over, she walked back to Tom and Alice.

"He said I need to go to the coroner's office and identify the bodies," she said with a whimper.

They got into Tom's vehicle and drove across town to the coroner, which also served as a funeral home. They were ushered to the basement. Four bodies were on tables with white sheets covering them.

Val followed the coroner to each body, where he slowly lifted the sheet off the body's head. She nodded as tears streamed down her cheeks. They went upstairs to the office for Val to sign forms that she identified the bodies.

Tom and Alice stood outside in the lobby with one of the funeral home directors.

"This is really tragic," the woman said.

"Oh, we know," Tom said. "We live next door. They were a great family."

"If only someone had checked on them earlier," the director said, "this might not have occurred."

"Huh? "What do you mean?" Tom had a perplexed look on his face.

"Our preliminary toxicology blood samples show that they were probably alive this morning."

"Alive?"

"They were overcome by the carbon monoxide but probably were in a deep sleep until around noon."

Tom stared at Alice. He didn't say a word.

Downtown Frankfort, KY

Accommodation

Richard Taylor

The wasp that nests in my mailbox
has offered a truce.
She doesn't sting.
I don't swat her papery comb.
So far our messages
have required no postmarks.

Mailbox ... with something inside?

From the Mind of Doc (My semi truck wreck of 1984)

Dennis "Doc" Martin

Early morning phone calls made:
"There was a wreck…", "I'm not sure…, "Hospital…."

Wrecked and thrown from the cab. Pinned against a tree.
Broken, bleeding and in shock.
Two hours for them to extract me from under the wheels of
The truck as it pins me against the tree…
Blood in my eyes. I can't see…

"No ambulance!" "Where is that ambulance!" I hear them
shout…"Get him to the E.R.!"
Only thing available is a funeral home's hearse. They take
me in a hearse…
"Talk to me" the driver says, "We are almost there…"
Blood in my eyes. I can't see…

Wheeled into the E.R. Shock wearing off. Can't move my
arm…
Yelling doctors. Yelling nurses and medical staff.
The sounds I hear as I lie there…
Blood in my eyes. I can't see…

They cut off my clothes. They draw blood and then more
blood.
A doctor says: "Talk to me", "can you hear me?"…
"Yes. Yes I can." I say as I lie there…
Blood in my eyes. I can't see…

X-ray, X-ray, X-ray. Surgery times two. Intensive care.
Pain.
Family arrives, worried. I hear them crying. They hold my
hand.
They say: "Love you, son". "Love you, honey." "We are
here…"
Can't see them. Blood in my eyes…

The days go by. I return to my home. Slowly walking on
my own.
Can't move my left arm. It is paralyzed.
Go to bed. Stay in bed. Rest. Heal. Rest.
I hear my daughter, love of my life, asking her mother:
"Why can't daddy hold me?…"

As I lie there in bed, I can't see her…
Tears in my eyes…

Making Biscuits

Dennis "Doc" Martin

It is early morning as I stand at the side of the kitchen door my face pressed against the old door trim, its cracked paint feeling rough against my skin, the old, yet very clean, linoleum flooring is cold upon my bare feet as I watch. Quietly standing there, I watch this woman I call mom as she makes biscuits for breakfast. She has not noticed me observing her — back then in late 1958 — yet I am there...

The drum stove which stands upon the metal stove mat in the kitchen is hot. Perhaps Mom or my dad may have put some coal into it before I awoke and I notice an edge or two at the top of the stove are glowing red. The kitchen is warm, toasty — some would say hot — as I watch my mom standing at the old kitchen counter adding flour and milk into the large crock mixing bowl. The contents are combined by her using a big wooden spoon until they become a firm dough. She is humming softly to herself as she labors and she soon places the spoon aside. I see this. I hear this.

The biscuit dough mixture is removed from the bowl and she places it onto a heavily-flour-dusted countertop. Then by hand, she kneads and mashes this dough all about the countertop. With the old wooden rolling pin, which, if memory serves, was one she got from her mother, she begins to flatten out the dough. There must be enough dough for about two dozen biscuits. She then uses an old tin can which — at one time — may have contained Early Days Peas, the top of course has been removed, the paper label soaked off and removed, and knife holes punched into its bottom end to allow air to escape, Mom deftly cuts out the circular biscuit shapes from the dough. I hear muffled whooshing sounds as puffs of air from the top of the can vent out from under Mom's hand. In the kitchen's light I notice tiny particles of flour swirling in the air above her hands and head as she cuts the dough.

A well-used baking pan, its sides blackened by years of biscuit baking, is placed onto a clean spot on the counter. Mom then removes the top of a silver can of lard that is always a staple in her kitchen. She then spoons out a large dollop of lard, plops it into the pan and, by hand, begins to smear the bottom and sides of the pan. She lard-coats the baking pan with a practiced ease of the knowledgeable baker that she is. There will be no baked biscuit dough sticking on this pan. I notice from where I stand that the baking pan is full, must be about two dozen...

Mom's old oven is pre-heated and she opens the door; I can imagine its heat as it rushes from that open door to combine with the heat of the old drum stove in her kitchen. Mom brushes back her hair so it don't singe and places the pan of biscuits inside. She checks her watch, noting the time. She will check the oven to see when the baking may be done —

caus' cause her old oven don't have a timer. She has just got to know by her watch when they are done, or close to it.

Still I stand by the door, her second son, and I continue to watch her as she works, while my little bare feet are chilled to the bone on the old linoleum-covered floor of our farm house in Shelby County, KY. Maybe I sniffle. Perhaps I shuffle my cold feet and with this movement or a sound, she spies me there at the kitchen doorway and says with a smile:

"Good morning, honey! I love you! Are you hungry? Breakfast will be ready in just a few minutes…"

Corner of Broadway and St. Clair Streets, Frankfort, KY

Red River Gorge

for Helen

Richard Taylor

Hiking along a ridgetop called Auxier Trail,
I look out across the vastness to other ridgetops,
between them a deep depression
through which runs a thread of water
I cannot see or even confidently name.

Gazing across the void,
I see other ridges, glints of light lifting
from the canteens of other hikers,
picking up bits of their voices — no words —
when the wind is right. Or wrong.
Above the ocher formations of rocks —
the earth's bones — is a blanket of gray
and clumps of bronze on oaks
whose jagged leaves just won't let go.

Richard Taylor

As we pass along the trail
following the etiquette of those in high places,
other hikers halt or excuse their passing
with a polite hello or muttered sorry.

Under an overhang, I find a trim Asian man
in a topaz jacket, camera in hand.
He shoots a fringe of icicles
at the ledge's lip, swords that drip
as the day warms. Our own lives
are also swords of ice melting,
held for a crystalline moment
in the flux of things — the flashing of metal
and flecks of broken speech,
accumulating on the dark sheen
of rocks below, rivulets of frost
working their way to a stream
whose name I do not know.

Bridge over Kentucky River

The Outpost

Damian C. Beach

The evening mist swirling around the man emerging from the restaurant's side door parted as he stepped onto the cluttered sidewalk. Buttoning his cashmere coat, Robert Allen Lamb scowled, sniffing the air, judging it like he did all things before him. His delicate nostrils were repulsed by the stench of the street, mixtures of sweat, grease, and the foul odors of the sewers. Grimacing, he grasped his solid silk scarf which usually engulfed his delicate neck. With one flick of his fingertips, the soft cloth covering his neck swirled around his face. Lamb sucked in the air filling his lungs with the sweet aroma of fresh vanilla blotting out the street. Although Mr. Robert Allen Lamb was of considerable girth, he carried his weight well, and has his tailored suits made with extra room for expansion. Mr. Robert Allen Lamb, famed food critic for the prestigious *Gastromene* newsletter, who with the slightest flick of his pen could close a restaurant in hours and had done so on many occasions.

Mr. Lamb stood and waited

Waiting and patience were not virtues usually associated with Mr. Robert Allen Lamb. But Mr. Lamb knew this moment was going to be worth it. He was waiting for the proprietor of the restaurant he had just examined. The owner had something he wanted and Mr. Lamb always got what he wanted. His house was filled with objects of his affection that had been desired and then acquired.

Mr. Lamb, hummed, Chopin's "Funeral March" grinning beneath his mask, thinking, relishing the moment like the sweet bouquet of a fine wine just before it touches your tongue.

"Mr. Lamb?" Robert Allen Lamb turned to examine his latest victim, Mr. Phillip Andre, owner of Andre's, supposedly a restaurant of some repute. He was a short, thin man in his late fifties with thinning salt-and-pepper black hair, black suit, white shirt, and black tie. On his coat cuffs he wore bands of gold braid, a symbol of his status as a chef. But now as Mr. Lamb gazed down at Andre's trembling lip and sweaty brow, he looked more like a petulant school boy waiting for his grades. "Was your meal pleasing?"

"No," Robert Allen Lamb said, looking at his well-polished fingernails. He stared at Mr. Andre with disgust. "The veal was inadequate, the vegetables were unsatisfactory, and the wine was flat."

"I shall see to it at once," the man said bowing, hoping that was the end, but he knew that it was not. Experience had taught Mr. Andre that Mr. Lamb enjoyed letting the guillotine blade slide ever so slowly, knowing only Mr. Lamb could stop the blade's descent. But he also knew the price for salvation would be high.

Mr. Lamb, tearing the scarf from his face, stuck his index finger into Mr. Andre's face, bellowing "Mr. Andre, your crème caramel was a pile of congealed filth. The caramel was a slimy mud mess. The custard was the color of sludge and tasted as though it had been boiling in someone's boot. And the glaze was a mass of burnt sugar with hunks of charcoal left. I dare say it may take me days, months before I am able to cleanse my palate of the horrid flavor." Lamb enjoyed watching the quivering man seeing a lifetime of work disappear in seconds.

"I have never been so revolted. Your restaurant should be replaced with a taco stand."

"Mr. Lamb, please," Mr. Andre begged. "Give me another chance."

Robert Allen Lamb returned his scarf over his mouth, concealing his thin smile. Closing his eyes, he began thumbing through his mind as to his demands. Satisfied he had kept the quivering man waiting long enough, Mr. Lamb said most insincerely. "Come now, Andre. Maybe your chef was having a bad night. Perhaps I could be persuaded."

"Oh," Andre bowing to Lamb, touching his hand. "I would be ever so grateful."

"How grateful?" Lamb loved this moment, wishing he could record it so he could enjoy it over and over again, but he knew the authorities would never understand. So, he had to savor it like the memory of food, with each and every flavor dancing around his mouth and across his sensitive tongue.

Then there was wine. Wine with its infinite varieties of flavors and styles and aromas. He remembered sitting in an old wine cellar as a child, closing his eyes and much to the delight of his grandfather, a master sommelier, being able to pick out each wine. It was there his grandfather gave him the choice. "Robert, food is life. If you pursue it, everything else is death." He chose.

Lamb, looking at the man, said in a calm clear voice, "You must choose- life or death."

"Life or death?" the man said, shaking his head. "I do not understand."

"I noticed in your cellar, hidden with some inferior California vintages, a bottle of Chateau Marganx 1787 marked with "TJ." Mr. Lamb knew the bottle was from the cellars of Thomas Jefferson. There were only ten left and he wanted one. "If that bottle were to find its way into my cellar by tomorrow morning no later than eight AM, I would forget this night. Otherwise."

"Mr. Lamb, you ask too much," Andre fretted. "That bottle has been in my family for over one hundred years. It was to be opened when my grandson married."

"No matter," Lamb looked up at the classic sign that glowed blue in the darkening sky. Mr. Lamb said scowling "Yes, Andre's taco shop should fit nicely over that sign without too much trouble."

Chuckling softly, Mr. Lamb began to slowly walk away counting each step. In his experience he never made it to ten before hearing the flutter of the white flag of surrender.

"All right, Mr. Lamb, you shall have your bottle."

"Excellent," Mr. Lamb said, not turning around. He didn't want Andre to see the wolfish delight on his face. The thought of Andre's anguish in having to part with such a prize sent orgasmic shivers across his body. "Deliver it to my butler. He will notify me if you change your mind."

It had been Lamb's intention to get the bottle no matter

what Andre served. To that end he drove his own car so that there would be no witnesses to the extortion. This way Andre presents a gift to the butler who in turn deposits in the cellar. Mr. Lamb knew the butler's lips were sealed. He had a file in his safe full of the butler's nasty little sins. Sins that authorities and the media love to smear around so that even an innocent man is damned.

Hurrying across the street, Mr. Lamb shielded his nose, hoping to quickly escape the foul stench of the streets. Suddenly his exposed left nostril caught a wisp of fragrance.

There it was floating high above the flotsam and jetsam of the stained concrete—a sweet fragrance. It was like seeing a delicate flower blooming on a field of carnage, small and innocent with its own light and universe in a land of ugly. Turning his face like a radar scope, Mr. Lamb closed his eyes and inhaled deeply-he let the air flow past his nostrils, his lungs. His brain began sorting through the scents, accepting only the pleasing, blotting out everything else. Finally, he found the scent and began breaking down the parts. Like an intricate puzzle, Mr. Lamb began reassembling it.

All food is made of parts or ingredients. In this case, the parts were easy to identify: sugar, flour, chocolate, and amaretto. But like all things simple, how they were assembled was the key to greatness or mediocrity. Anybody could make a chocolate cake, but very few could make it into something so elegant and grand to fetch one hundred thousand a slice at Christie's and very few deserved it.

Mr. Robert Allen Lamb knew he deserved it all by any means. Swearing an oath and following his nose like a bloodhound, he came to a man on the street corner holding a simple white box.

"What have you there?" Lamb said, pointing at the

white box.

"This trifle," the man said, his face hidden in the dark shadow. "It is a gift for Mr. Garrett Madison."

"Mr. Madison," Lamb said trying hard not to grab the box from the man's hands. The fragrance was over powering, driving every sense in his body to the point of overload. "The food critic for the Times."

"Yes," the man said shaking his head in agreement. "He agreed to sample a meal at my new restaurant. I brought this as a gesture of good will."

"What do you have?" Lamb said, seeing an opportunity.

"Oh," the man said, glancing into the box. "On one side I have a truffle and on the other a simple French dessert. A tarte Tatin."

Lamb's stomach almost erupted in joy. Very few people on the earth had really enjoyed the ultimate joy of the perfection reached by biting into the sweet creamery taste of the apple hidden within delicate pastry that was a tarte Tatin.

"I do wish Mr. Madison would hurry," the man said, looking up and down the nearly deserted street. "He said he would be here at nine and it is almost nine-ten."

"Perhaps, I could be of assistance," Lamb said, his fingers twitching with raw emotion at the thought of two desserts. "I am Robert Allen Lamb. Perhaps you have heard of me?"

"Yes," the man said. "I was going to ask you but I didn't think you would be interested."

"What kind of restaurant?" Lamb said, still eyeing the white box and dreaming of its contents.

"It's called THE OUTPOST. We serve wild game. Meat." He paused, looking first at the box and then at Mr.

Lamb, "most people don't normally consume quail, venison, rabbit, and bison."

"Quail? Very few know how to prepare quail."

"My Mother was of French descent," the man said, looking at the box. "She taught me everything about cooking and the preparation of specialty dishes like quail and other meats. Some need hours, sometimes even days or weeks to prepare."

"So, you know how to prepare quail?" Mr. Lamb said, remembering his grandfather's hunting lodge. His grandfather was not only a wine merchant but a master hunter, killing quail and pheasant. He remembered sitting across from his grandfather as the logs in the fireplace popped and cracked, matching the sound of the quail's bones cracking beneath his teeth. Preparing quail took both skill and patience.

Mr. Robert Allen Lamb eyed the man, smiling like a spider watching a fly.

"I'll tell you what, young fellow," Lamb said. "Normally I charge to review a new restaurant but I'm feeling generous and I'll do it for free."

"Are you sure?" the man said. "Mr. Madison?"

"See here. Do you want your restaurant to succeed or fail? If you prepare a fine meal, my review will almost guarantee your outstanding success. Make up your mind."

"Of course I want to succeed. Everything is riding on it," the young man said reluctantly. "I would be most grateful."

"Then let's go," Lamb said, his mind racing as to how to turn grateful into slavery. "My car is over there. You lead and I'll follow."

"No," the man said shaking his head. "I'll take you

there. I've already had three people try to steal my recipes. If any person saw you and your fancy car pull up who knows what would happen. My truck is right over there. Of course, if you disagree there's always Mr. Madison."

Lamb thought for a minute, quickly sizing up the situation. It had all the elements he relished—a desperate man betting everything on his restaurant. And he knew this buffoon had just the right amount of gullibility to fall easily into his extortion trap. Robert Allen Lamb knew it added up to a lifetime of blackmail and slavery served up by his own gourmet chef. He could not refuse the temptation.

"Lead the way."

"Very well," the man said, opening the door to his truck. "This will be an unforgettable night."

"I hope so," Mr. Lamb said, entering the truck's cab and reclining on the soft leather seat. "Or you will regret it."

"A great meal is carefully planned," the man said, handing Mr. Lamb the white box. "Try the truffle first."

Lamb sniffed the delicate pastry, letting the tip of his tongue just barely kiss the light sugarcoating. It was like licking an angel's wing, the swirl of flavors so intense as to take Mr. Lamb's breath. Never had he had such a truffle. He nibbled the crust like a mouse, each bite washing across his palate in a rainbow of flavors. When Mr. Lamb had consumed the last morsel, he felt tears of joy in his eyes.

"Young man," Robert Allen Lamb finally was able to gasp. "That was magnificent."

"I'm glad you approve," the young man said, handing Mr. Lamb a small fork wrapped in a silk napkin.

"Before you taste the tarte Tatin I suggest you cleanse your palate."

"I would, but have nothing."

The man revealed a small silver thermos after stopping the truck on the side of the road under a street lamp. "What kind of host would I be if I did not supply everything. But I must insist you wear the safety harness before we go any further."

"Where are we going?"

"I'm sorry, the road to the restaurant is not quite finished and it gets a little bumpy for those not used to it."

"See here."

"If you're uncomfortable with it, I can always ask Mr. Madison," the man said, removing the box from Lamb's hands. "I'm sure he would like the taste of the Tatin."

Lamb, looking at the young man, was about to decline when a whisper of the truffle came back and like a fairy danced on his tongue. It was like a siren's song luring him to crash on the rocks of pleasure. He had to surrender, the thought of the Tatin could not be denied, yet he could not allow Madison to sneer at him.

"I suppose the benefits will outweigh the discomfort." Lamb said as the man helped him put on the restraint. Lamb's mind now was full of plots and schemes. He was way beyond blackmail as the flavors of the truffle still lingered. Evil swirled in Mr. Lamb's mind as he secretly glanced at the young man and thought, "His impudence shall be punished. No one makes a fool out of Robert Allen Lamb. He shall be crushed."

"I see you're enjoying yourself."

"How so?"

"You were smiling," the man said, uncapping the thermos. The truck's cab immediately filled with the sweet, sharp aroma of expresso coffee. "Sip it slowly," the young man said as he handed the silver cup to Lamb. "It's my mother's favorite recipe. Reserved for only the finest palates."

Lamb did as he was instructed, letting the liquid flow slowly across his tongue as he swirled it around his mouth. It was rich, hot, and soothing at the same time. Lamb closed his eyes, letting every one of his senses indulge as he felt the liquid pouring into his body, its silky fingers coating every organ with velvety smoothness. In seconds Mr. Lamb felt as though he were bathing in warm oil, every muscle relaxing. Sip by sip, Mr. Lamb felt his body drifting away.

In minutes Mr. Lamb had consumed almost the entire thermos and desired more, neglecting the Tatin.

"What is this coffee?" Lamb said, starting to notice his tongue did not seem to want to work right. "It is making me feel a bit drunk, but I like it."

"It is the extract of the hibiscus flower you are feeling," the young man said, not taking his eyes off the ever-darkening road, before adding, "You who are rich and whose troubles are few will soon come to see my point of view."

"What balderdash," Lamb said, licking the last dregs of coffee from the cup. "What do you mean? You and I have nothing in common. Your point of view? I am Robert Allen Lamb and you're a mere peasant."

"Do you remember when you were eighteen you and your grandfather were hunting. Across a field you saw a young girl of thirteen playing with a lamb. Do you?"

"Yes, vaguely. We discovered she was simple-minded. What of it?"

"Do you remember what happened next?"

"Yes, my grandfather, after examining the animal, inquired about buying it. It was of exquisite texture and musculature and he offered a fair price, but this peasant man came screaming at us. He had no right to do that. Grandfather chastised him for showing disrespect to gentlemen."

"By whipping him and tying him to a tree after you both raped the girl."

"What of it," Lamb slurred. "We left adequate compensation for the lamb."

"She was my sister."

"So, she was deflowered by gentlemen rather than some grimy peasant boy. She probably lives in a shack with her eight or nine bottom-feeding brats."

"No," the man said, glancing at Lamb. "She is chef of fine meats."

"Tonight's meal better be good," Lamb said. "I am not someone to be trifled with."

"Oh, it will be," the man said laughing.

Far off in the distance, shimmery lights cut the murky darkness. The Outpost was far off the roadway, hidden by a forest of thick pine and cedar trees. Beyond the trees, low in the sky was a yellow moon glowing, showing the way, playing hide and seek with the cloud of grey smoke coming from the restaurant's chimney.

Two days later.

The Outpost restaurant opened to sparkling reviews written in the online edition of the Times by esteemed critic Mr. Garrett Madison. Mr. Madison raved about the delicacy of the cuisine, especially the special wild game stew whose flavor and sweetness of the meat no one could identify. Mr. Madison wrote "the crème caramel was a delight to the eyes and the tongue."

On another note, the Times reported the disappearance

of critic Robert Allen Lamb. A Mr. Andre of Andre's restaurant reported that Mr. Lamb was not at his residence. Mr. Andre went there to thank Mr. Lamb for his glowing review of Mr. Andre's restaurant.

"It seems, according to the online edition of the Times, Mr. Lamb is a missing person that no one misses," the young man said, reading his phone, sitting on the edge of the bed where a recumbent figure lay. Oxygen tubes prevented the figure from speaking. Straps across his chest restricted the figure's movement.

"I know you can hear me, Mr. Robert Allen Lamb. Thanks to your contributions, the restaurant's opening was a grand success. And in the future, you will be contributing other items of interest. Rest well. I will check in on you from time to time. I trust my sister will take good care you. You took so much from her, it's the least she can do for you. Rest well, Mr. Robert Allen Lamb." The young man chuckled as he turned off the light and closed the door.

In the dark, strapped to the bed, the moaning figure made his restraints jingle. There was little else he could do — with no arms, no legs, no tongue, and no eyes.

Fort Hill

Ugliest is the Best

Rachana Rahman

Ugliest, But the Best Cookie You've Ever Eaten, written on the poster inside the office hallway, jolted me to a stop.

Under the poster an extremely attractive young lady was sitting at a small fold-out table with some cookies lying on aluminum foil. Her low-cut dress, shiny red shoes, model-size breasts and tight hips, movie-style blonde hairdo, false lashes and her self-assured sensual postures, giving the passers by a clear message: this saleswoman is knowledgeable about beauty, sexiness and success.

Every Friday, just before lunch break, someone from the staff would sit at a table offering homemade goodies, mostly just for fun. Sometimes I stop by to collect brownies, muffins, cakes or cookies for my child.

So, I looked at the cookies and there was no doubt—those cookies were not impressive. I couldn't verify whether they were meant to be circles, squares or ovals. The deep, dark unappealing brown color couldn't attract me, and I couldn't detect what that gooey and mushy filling was, peeking out from the middle of each cookie.

Gosh! They were ugly, I said to myself.

Ugliest, But the Best Cookie You've Ever Eaten. I read the poster again. This time I noticed someone had underlined the word *best* with a green marker, trying to give the assurance to the buyers that these ugly cookies contained the best taste.

Could it be?

The pretty saleswoman scanned me from top to bottom, critically checking my worn-out Walmart shoes, the skirt my mom sent me from my country, and my untrimmed black hair, which complimented my olive complexion. Her unsmiling blue eyes lingered on my black eyes. She appeared to be trying to decide whether I was Mexican, Latino or Indian. She turned with her disgusted look on her face, as if I were as hopeless and as ugly as her cookies.

Quickly, the nice-looking lady with the ugly cookies became surrounded by customers, mainly men, mostly white men. It was clear these men wanted to support the ugliness of her cookies and at the same time the prettiness of an American beauty.

While I was standing near the table, very few of the men even looked at me, and, when they did, I received the same message: you are foreign and pathetic in comparison with the American Beauty—you are as ugly as those cookies. Their eyes were fixed upon the white flesh of that woman, as if she had hypnotized them; if she would say, "Let's invade the Island!" they would do it without any hesitation.

How did she do that? I pondered.

With great amazement, I was witnessing a huge sale of ugliness, or, should I say, the propaganda of American prettiness. Most of the cookies were gone in ten minutes; most were bought by men, mainly white men.

Only when four or five cookies remained…

"Aren't you going to buy some?" the persuasive blonde asked me.

She, I bet, had never experienced the ugly part of life. Otherwise, she wouldn't have looked at me that way or wouldn't have chosen the word *Ugliest* so boldly on her poster.

I looked at the cookies again. They were still ugly, extremely ugly; deliberately made to be ugly; exposing their ugliness openly, nakedly and indefensibly. I could feel those ugly cookies; I started seeing me and the immigrants at the border — warped with aluminum blankets as those cookies. That gooey and mushy filling in the middle of each cookie reminded me of one's past history, screaming — help me, understand me — waiting to be judged for worthiness by the self-loving society.

"Aren't you going to buy any?" she asked me again.

I searched for the ugliest and picked it up — the one which, if Mr. President would command me to take a bite of that cookie, otherwise he would send me back to my country or lock me up or shoot me as an immigrant, swear I would not eat that cookie.

She was only taking cash; I only had enough for one. I took the cookie home.

"It is written that this is the ugliest cookie, but best in taste. Try this cookie and let me know if it is the best one," I told my ten-year-old son, whose taste buds were young and fresh. He could scan and find any vegetables I had deliberately hidden inside the meatballs and lasagna made for him.

I waited for a 'yuck', 'ugh', 'ick', 'eww' sound, but…

"COOKIE!" His eyes sparkled with a great joy like those

of Cookie Monster on Sesame Street. With great care, he tenderly carried the cookie to the sofa. He checked the cookie from all sides; its odd size, disagreeable brown color and the untraceable gooey and mushy filling in the middle didn't bother him. The innocent and pure child couldn't find any ugliness in that cookie. He wiggled around until he was comfortable on the sofa. He opened his mouth and prepared himself to get a big bite of that cookie, which by now had lost all its ugliness.

I closed my eyes. *Please God, let this innocence and purity remain generation after generation, let this cookie be the best; and let our ugliness perish*, I prayed.

Kentucky River Lock

From the Dark

Pamela Hirschler

As if I could know any place,
I drag my roots, leaving
a keeled trough on the river bank.

We paddle against the current,
the bow of the canoe slices
beyond where I have been, beyond
where I know, beyond
where I need to belong.

Easter-egg Hunt

A Memoir
Circa 1961-62

Dennis "Doc" Martin

The fist which struck the left side of my buzz-cut head was attached to the right arm of a chubby young classmate of mine, and he had put some weight behind the punch.

He and I are first grade classmates in the Shelby County, Kentucky school system, (Glennerie), and along with thirty or so other first graders, we have been allowed out on the schoolyard property for the annual "Easter Egg Hunt." Many of us have been waiting this day for weeks, ever since our teacher first advised us what was going to happen on this day!

My classmates and I are standing shoulder to shoulder in a line looking out over the grounds, while in our hands are the containers which we have "created" in class to hold our found colored eggs. Some of the containers are simple brown paper grocery sacks that we brought from home and they have been colored with crayons. Lots of yellow, green and blues, some tulips can be seen depicted on a couple of the bags. There were two "well off" children who brought in dyed yellow pillow cases and they had painted flowers, hills and the sky upon them. Their sacks look really nice. One of the boys forgot his sack and our teacher rummaged around in the coat room and found a small cardboard shoe-box and gave it to him to use.

A cool spring breeze is blowing the hem of our teacher's dress as she stands to our front and speaks to us of the "can do and can't do" of this event. Some of my classmates stand rigid and listen intently, while others are looking all around the school grounds and swinging their sacks side to side.

The early spring grasses of the schoolyard have yet to be mowed. The bright, deep green of the grass and their height are perfect hiding places for the numerous, hard-boiled Easter eggs which have been hidden on the grounds in front of us. Looking around, I have spied in the distance some bright yellows and reds among the clumps of grass and make ready to get them first!

Upon looking down at my feet and just to my left, in a small hollow of green grass, I see an egg. It is light blue in color, with a thin yellow stripe around its middle. The shell has some small cracks in it, probably it was stepped on by one of my less-observant classmates. Though the shell is damaged it still counts after the hunt is over and back in class, we total who has the most eggs. Slowly I look up and notice my classmate to my left has also seen the egg and he edges to his right getting closer. I move to my left getting closer still.

Dennis "Doc" Martin

Our teacher yells "GO!" and most of the line springs forward in a mad rush towards the grounds and the hidden eggs—all except two young boys who are soon in a battle royal - over one cracked Easter egg—light blue in color, with a small yellow stripe. Immediately upon hearing "GO", I quickly bent down and with my left hand snatched that cracked egg from the ground.

My classmate balled his right fist and punched me upon the side of my head and the fight was on! He punched and I returned the punches. We grappled. Some buttons were torn from my shirt. He hooked my leg with his leg and we both tumbled to the ground, rolling and punching for all we are worth. The dampness of the early spring ground could be felt on our bare skin and through our clothing, which soon became severely grass-stained.

Our teacher and another adult soon came to break up the scuffle and from the ground he and I are pulled apart and up to our feet. We two combatants are huffing and puffing trying to catch our collective breath, while off in the distance, the rest of our class are locating all the eggs and placing them into their colorful containers.

My antagonist and I stand by our teacher, with our grass-stained shirts and pants, both of us holding empty, torn and wrinkled brown paper grocery sacks as we look at the squashed remnants of a light blue colored Easter egg on the mashed and scuffed grass where we fought.

The Importance of Words

Pamela Hirschler

You are the only one —

his half smile
    fence rows
        clothes lines
the neighbor's pickup
    grave yards
        coyotes
the cloud of starlings overhead
    hay bales
        tobacco knives
the jet trailing its stream like a meteor —

left to remember.

Narthex

Terre Brothers

There's something that runs through your bones that turns your blood to ice. You feel the trickle of sweat pouring down the back of your neck and your stomach feels like a stone. You must stand, because you are the one being judged, and you must be on your feet to hear your sentence. Whatever the judge says, that's your future. You know that you are innocent. You know you couldn't even bear to think of what they have accused you of doing. And you know that none of that matters.

You stand there, and your blood is cold in your veins. Maybe being cold means you're numb, and you won't hurt so bad when you hear those words that you've been dreading, that you've heard before in night terrors that wake you up in a freezing sweat, your heart beating right out of your chest. You've heard the words before, so why do they come as such a shock when they're announced? Why do you have to grab the heavy wooden chair arms behind you not to fall?

You look around the courtroom and try to find the face of your husband. There he is, in the gallery. You stare at him hard, searching his face for an opening, a way for you to think the words hard enough for him to accept them. *I didn't do it.* But he looks right back at you like you could be a stranger on the street. There's not even tears or sadness about the baby girl, cold and stiff in a pine box under the ground. You hear them announce the sentence, and you hear your counsel argue for leniency in the sentence. Leniency? You want to scream, leniency? How about acquittal? Because I didn't do it. You look down though, and avoid everyone's eyes. Nothing will get you anything to break down screaming and crying here. They already think you're a cold, hard killer. Either that or a dangerous crazy woman. None of them are taking your side. You stand there while you are discussed like a nameless, faceless menace in a lunatic asylum or a prisoner of war. Which one shall it be? You can't even feign interest in what will happen to you now. All you know is that your baby girl died and you have been convicted of killing her.

You are led away by two prison matrons and taken into an antechamber. It is all gray, like your life from now on. You sit at the heavy table and wait for your counselor. When he comes in, he is red in the face and hoarse from arguing. He lost though, and now he can't look you in the face. When you catch his eye, you realize that he thinks you are guilty just like everyone else. He is more upset that he did not win his case; granting freedom to the mother who killed her own baby would have made quite a story at the club. He tells you that it has been arranged for you to go to a penitents' refuge, and this doesn't sound as bad as prison or hard labor in a workhouse so you press your lips together in a grim smile and thank him, "your lord." He reaches out to shake your hand and then thinks better of it and withdraws it, while

you look helplessly to the side. He summons the prison matrons who drive you alone in an armored bus as if you were
fifty inmates to the "refuge," a convent run by the Sisters.
It's a cold-looking building and you try to take small comfort in the fact it's not a prison. You know what they do to
baby-killers in a women's prison, because the lunatic in the
cell next to yours whispers it to you every night through the
bars, her lisp sounding less like a voice and more like a ser-
pent's hiss.

The prison matrons lead you inside the large front
doors. They slam shut like a prison cell and you startle like
a frightened mouse. The matrons pull you roughly, remind-
ing you that you are not here for anything you have a right
to have feeling about. They pull you to the admitting Sister,
who calls the Mother Superior in. The Mother Superior
takes one look at you and dismisses the prison matrons. She
makes light of their protestations, and another Sister comes
into the room and shows the matrons out. Only then does
Mother Superior sit down and really study you.

She asks you if you know what crime you have committed.

You open your mouth to protest, you have committed
no crime.

Mother Superior holds up her hand, and already she has
taught you obedience. You shut your mouth.

She asks you if you understand what infanticide means.

You nod, and a tear comes, unbidden. It flows down
your face which is already raw and chapped from crying for
the last week... or has it been two? You have lost track of
time as well as your soul.

Mother Superior turns to the admitting Sister. See, she
says. She is showing remorse. That's a good thing. We may

be able to help this poor soul understand her grave sins and begin to repent.

You try not to let another tear fall. You know you didn't commit this sin, or any crime. You want to shake her and scream, *I didn't do it, I loved her, I would never do it, I am a good mother.* But you keep silent, because you know none of this matters anymore. You are where you are, convicted and ready to pay the price.

Mother Superior is saying something about hard work being the beginning of your repentance. She does not offer confession, nor does she want to hear you speak. You are told that there is a strict code of conduct here which benefits the spiritual growth of all the women here, including silence, prayer and working to earn your keep in the laundry the asylum operates. You are told to pray for your very soul.

You realize that's not worth praying for.

You then step into the place they have sentenced you to. You work, you pray, you rarely speak. No one really asks you why you are there. Occasionally you get some strange looks from the women who are large with child, but they just assume you are a woman who has already given up your baby into the orphanage for adoption, and you become just another faceless, nameless, shapeless figure in this grayscale of a world. You sometimes cry yourself to sleep in your cot until a voice in the darkness tells you hush. And you don't try to be anything other than a cog in the machine that keeps the laundry running.

Days are all the same, and nights are all at once too long and yet painfully brief. You think of your children, out there in the world being raised by your husband's woman-kin, mother and sister, and you wonder if your children miss you. Or do they believe what everyone says about you?

It's thinking on this, late at night, that finally gets to you. You have heard the other women talk about how long they have to be in this place, and when they plan to leave. You know that you have no escape, no release, no date that your sentence will end. You think of your children, the only things you've ever loved and you realize that you are never going to see them, and they are never going to want to see you. It's thinking on this, knowing this, that finally drives you to it.

You know it's a mortal sin. You know it means your soul will go to hell. You no longer care. You filch the key to the roof from one of the younger Sister's pockets, and you wait until the dormitories are dark. You rise, not bothering to put on a dressing gown over the thin nightgown you've been given to sleep in. Where you're going, you won't feel cold for long. You look around the other cots, making sure the other women are fast asleep. You can hear one of the younger girls snoring to herself and you think of your oldest, Sally, and her breathing whenever her asthma was acting up and you cry some more.

You get up and make your way in bare feet to the corridor and then to the small stairway in the back of the dormitory hall. You fumble with the key, but still keep silent enough not to wake anyone. You open the door and climb the frozen iron spiral staircase to the roof.

Once you are on the top of the building, you can look out and see the lights of Cork as well as the dark island of the asylum to which you have been committed in this life. The wind blows strong and cold, an icy sleet coming in from the Sea. You shudder and fight the temptation to run back down the staircase and to your dormitory, denying that you came out here at all. Then you remember that nothing is going to change, nothing at all, and so you stride quickly to the edge of the roof and look down at the cobblestones of the courtyard, shining like black diamonds because they are frosted with ice. You feel glad that those stones are far enough to break you irreparably and send you to hell once you step off into nothingness. You make ready for this step. You cross yourself and then you chide yourself. What use does God have of you? Why are you blessing yourself when you are already damned? And you step with one foot -

And then Eileen O'Malley, that child who lives in fantasy, pulls you roughly back to the safety of the rooftop. She calls it bringing you back to reality.

As if she had any idea what that means.

Cove Spring Park

Toy Soldiers Entrenched on a Root-cellar

A Memoir

Dennis "Doc" Martin

The trenches are dug with an old soup spoon. Toy soldiers positioned within, row after row.
"Boom, Ka-Boom!!" sounds the artillery, "Brrrrat a tat, tat, tat, tat, tat…" the machine guns roar.
"Forward! Fire! Onward men!!" are the shouts and sounds of my imagination.

A shadow darkens my imagined battlefield and I look up.
He stands there, my great-uncle, a veteran of the "War to End all Wars."
Silently watching a young boy play on the grassy slopes of a root cellar.

A tear slowly slides down his unshaven face,
As perhaps in a memory, he returns once again to a day, a place, "over there"
When - unlike my imagined battlefield –

It was real…

I Have Dyslexia but it Doesn't Have Me!

Barbara Yancey

Hi! My name is Melanie. School used to be a real bummer. I used to cry a lot and get frustrated. Learning the alphabet was even horrible. A lot of people confuse b and d. Me? If it can be twisted into another letter my brain would do it. I felt so stupid!

Numbers were almost as bad. 63 and 36 looked the same. Made me feel stupid again!

Then it happened. I got a second teacher. She showed me how to beat dyslexia. Yeah, I have dyslexia but it doesn't have me. This is my story.

Once upon a time I sat at my desk just looking at the letters of the alphabet on my paper. They just kept moving around. Letters like p and q or d and p or b and d, or even h would look like upside down. If it was possible to twist it, it twisted. I always liked the letters o and x because you can't twist them into something else!

One day a nice lady came to my classroom. My teacher said I would go and do some fun stuff with her. She was right. The nice teacher came and took me to her class. She told me her name was Ms. Flannery and when we got to her class there were other boys and girls. She told me their names. She told them mine. She told me she wanted me to read some letters to her. I looked around. The other kids were doing other things. Whew! Only she would know how dumb I was. I even told her I was dumb. She told me that I was not dumb. She said we all have challenges.

Challenges come in all different sizes and shapes. It's all up to us as to what we do about it. My challenge is dyslexia. My brain doesn't learn the same way as others. But that is okay. There are other ways of learning. Her job was to help me find the right path. My job was to learn it. It was my choice. Wow! To feel smart? Sure. I'll try! She smiled again. I like it when she smiles. It makes me feel good about myself.

So the work began. She listened to me struggle as I read. She gave me strategies to help me read. The same with math. I have strategies to help me keep the numbers straight. I can use my strategies anytime. Even on tests! Someday I may not need them. I already don't use them as much as I used to. Ms. Flannery says I'm also teaching myself strategies. I told her one day that sometimes when I'm asked a question, I go up to my brain where the filing cabinets are to find that all the files are scattered on the floor. She taught me how to turn those questions around to make them easier to find the right file.

I like writing on the computer. I can write down my ideas without worrying about how to put down the letters or words. The computer does that for me. It makes it easier to focus on what I want to write and getting ideas down. I like the computer period. I still work on writing letters on paper and so forth but that will come in time.

I have extra time to take tests. That's so I can use my strategies to do my best. Sometimes that takes longer than if I didn't have to use strategies. It's not cheating. It's leveling the playing field so I get the same chance as everyone else.

I'm not dumb. I learn differently and that's okay. Everyone is different, everyone is unique. That's what makes us special. If everyone had to learn my way, then they would need to have coping skills not me. I've learned a lot about myself. I have lots of strengths. My favorite one is figuring things out on the computer. I can even show Ms. Flannery how to do stuff on the computer. That's cool. I get to teach the teacher!

I'm also good at understanding things that I read. Sometimes, a teacher or another adult will read something to me and then ask questions about what was read. It's easier to understand if it's read to me and if I want part of it read again, it will be repeated.

Sometimes kids make fun of me. I know they're not my true friends. They have issues if they feel like they have to bully me to feel better. I try to ignore them the best I can. My real friends stick by me like I stick by them.

I like school now. Some things are hard. But that's okay. One of my friends hates science. I think science is cool. I help her understand some of the stuff we have to study. She helps me when I forget and write a letter backwards or write a number wrong. We both have problems with directions. We all have challenges to go along with our many strengths. We have to help each other.

Yes, I have dyslexia, but it doesn't have me!

Tamsin

Shannon McRoberts

Grey clouds hung against a blackened sky as the rain poured down. Droplets splashed onto the casket in front of her. Tamsin sat slack in the folding chair. Her hands fell loosely to her sides as she tilted her head up towards the sky. The rain pelted her expressionless face causing streaks of black mascara to run down her cheeks. Her blonde hair hung in wet clumps down her back. The service ended hours ago, but she couldn't find the energy to leave.

A cloaked figure stood watching Tamsin behind the seats under a row of old oak trees. Satisfied they were alone, the figure approached the grieving woman and sat in the chair behind her. The figure leaned her lips towards Tamsin's ear. "You summoned me, dear?"

The words hit Tamsin like ice. She never planned on hearing that voice again, but in a moment of weakness Tamsin summoned her. Tamsin's eyes shot open as she spun around in her seat. Her gaze landed on the cloaked figure, a woman with ice blue eyes and raven black hair.

"Adrestia, I didn't think you would come."

A weak smile crossed Adrestia's lips. "Come now, little assassin, when have I ever denied your requests? You begged to join my ranks and I welcomed you. You begged me to return your heart and release you. So, I did. Now, you cry out as a woman wronged and ask for my judgement. Here I am."

Tamsin hung her head and cast her gaze down to the ground. "I forsook you. I left you."

"I've come to those less worthy, why wouldn't I come to you?"

Tamsin lifted her head to meet Adrestia's gaze. "You said we were through."

"We were, but I never meant for it to be forever. I figured you'd live your happy little mortal life with that man and come back after you passed into the Great Beyond."

Tears flooded Tamsin's grey eyes while the weight of her thoughts caused her breath to grow shallow. "I gave up so much for this mortal life and now I have lost everything. They murdered him, Adrestia. I want vengeance!"

Adrestia reached out and stroked the top of Tamsin's head. "Shhh, child, you have lost nothing. It's only been ten years. That's merely a drop in the bucket of time. Besides, I can restore you."

"Restore me, how? As you pointed out, I've aged ten years and now I'm almost forty-two. I'm not fit for your service. I summoned you hoping you could assign one of your assassins to my cause."

"I stopped you from growing old while you worked for me for over twenty years, didn't I? What makes you think I can't turn back the hands of time?"

Tamsin bowed her head and sighed. "I'm sorry. It seems

I've lost faith in many things lately."

"Are you sure this is what you want? I won't be able to release you a second time. The ritual to restore you would cause your body to disintegrate if you tried to return to a mortal form again."

"As long as I may request one last thing."

Adrestia raised her brow and looked at Tamsin. "You don't really have the leeway to add requests. I'm already breaking several rules by coming here to the mortal plane."

Holding up her hand, Tamsin looked at Adrestia. "I want my heart buried with him. It was always his. It should stay with him. I won't need it anymore."

"If that is all you wish, I can accommodate that. Are you ready?"

Tamsin nodded and stood to walk towards the casket. She lifted the lid and peered inside one last time. Luke looked peaceful like he would wake up from his afternoon nap at any moment. Tamsin held her breath and waited for his chest to rise, but it never did. She smiled as she thought to herself. *The mortician did a good job reconstructing his neck. Most people didn't even realize his head had been severed.* She leaned in and pressed her lips to his. The cold from his corpse permeated Tamsin to her soul. It was a cold unlike any she had ever felt. Reaching for the buttons on her shirt she undid the first four exposing her chest. Turning around she found Adrestia waiting for her.

Adrestia took a deep breath and nodded. She plunged one hand into Tamsin's chest and pulled out her heart. With her other hand, Adrestia filled the gaping hole in Tamsin's chest full of magic. The wound closed in a matter of seconds. Adrestia handed the still-beating heart to Tamsin.

Tamsin turned and placed her heart in the casket with

Luke before shutting the lid. Adrestia's magic coursed through her body once again. The ten years Tamsin aged while mortal disappeared as she stood there watching Luke's casket descend into the grave. The remnants of Tamsin's mortal life now lay buried in the ground with her love. Free from the confinements of a mortal's heart, Tamsin vowed those responsible for her sadness would suffer.

Bridge at Devil's Hollow

no way to go back

Mark Kinnaird

remember that time
in the car
with bob seger playing on the radio
we already felt nostalgic
even though the moment wasnt over
then you talked a mile a minute
about nothing much
i laughed at you
you laughed at me
and we laughed at the idea
now
i wonder if we understood
the hardships that awaited
me with mine
you with yours
but didnt we know
we were just a fleeting moment
passing by on the road
headlights off
voices breezing by
and forgetting each other as we talked

Sun-dried Tomato Toast

Keith Hellard

It began with the radio.

Not that it was a particularly valuable radio, not even when it was given to him by his aunt and uncle as a graduation gift; it was one of those mid-range models easily found on the shelves of any big-box outlet, sometimes even in drugstores. Although it sported no fancy graphic equalizer, digital tuner, or other advanced controls, it had diligently seen him through four years of college, two years of graduate school, his first pigsty bachelor-pad apartment with James and Rodney downtown, the more upscale apartment he'd taken after landing his job at the plant, and, more recently, the condo where he and Wendy moved after their wedding. Never did it denounce, or applaud, his slow sojourn from heavy metal to classic rock, and eventually to easy listening. It simply soldiered on.

He'd risen then as he did every day, not to the sound of said radio, but the annoyingly-jaunty jingle from his alarm clock. It was 2:00 in the afternoon — a couple of hours before his shift at the plant began. After checking his phone for messages from the first shift managers, he showered, then made his way to the kitchen where he switched on the coffee pot, popped a plastic container of leftover spaghetti into the microwave, and decided he'd much rather listen to the relaxing sounds of 104.5 than the childish squabbling he'd no doubt encounter on any given television channel.

It was then — that moment — he would for so long remember, and struggle to recapture: the half-second of blissful unawareness preceding the beginning of the end, so to speak, before the first subtle chinks in the armor plating appeared. Leaning to press its worn silver power button, he was puzzled to find all that remained of the radio were black smudges streaked across the marble countertop by its dry-rotten rubber feet.

Wendy must have it, he decided, as he carried his coffee and spaghetti to the kitchen table. The radio at her office must have crapped out and she'd taken his until a new one could be purchased. Had she mentioned it to him? Working different shifts they rarely crossed paths anymore, their conversations consisting of little more than a hurried yes, no, or goodbye. In a somber silence he finished his spaghetti.

Again he rose to the increasingly-irritating jingle from his alarm clock, checked his phone for messages, climbed into the frigid bathtub, showered, and careened down the hallway towards the kitchen. Unlike that now-infamous late-summer day some twelve weeks prior, today he wrapped himself in a terrycloth robe and stepped onto the back deck. Leaning over the iron railing as far as he dared, he scoured the adjacent intersection. No children, no runners, no vagrants. Nothing but tendrils of steam rising like ghosts from nearby grates.

Back inside he scanned the living room — coffee table, bookcases, entertainment center, and curio cabinet. Nothing amiss. No newly-revealed dust rings. Even the pillows atop the sofa and the raggedy mohair throw draped across the recliner appeared undisturbed.

Anxiously he entered the kitchen — the part of his new daily ritual he both longed for and dreaded, the sight he couldn't face after a long shift at the plant and so postponed until he awakened, the five or so seconds which set the tone of his existence until this time tomorrow. Simultaneously his heart fluttered, and crumbled, soared heavenward like an escaped balloon, and thudded against the unyielding earth like a ball of ice.

The twenty he left under the coffee mug Wendy had bought at one of those tourist traps in Boca Raton was gone. It always was. At this he expressed neither surprise nor alarm. When nothing else was disturbed and the food he left for her remained untouched, the twenty always vanished. But, as the plate beside the mug and the twenty *was* today empty, perhaps she'd lingered a moment in the chair behind which he now stood, and thought things over. Perhaps some faint, tenuous thread of their bond might yet endure.

Unless it didn't, he sighed, his body wilting. Likely she'd come only for the money, and he was nothing more to her than an ATM. She was broke now, and desperate, having depleted her checking account a week or two after he discovered the termination notice from her office, and watched helplessly as her Volvo was repossessed. The radio was but a tell-tale symptom of that desperation — the bottom of a lonely ladder whose broken rungs he had passed daily for months and somehow overlooked. After the handbag he bought her in Vegas, the 40-piece silver service they received at their wedding reception, her jewelry box, tablet, nearly every article in her wardrobe, her bottles of designer perfumes, as well as several dozen crystal frogs she'd collected since middle school, there was little of value left she could secret out of the condo.

His thoughts racing like disturbed ants, he turned from the table to the counter where the radio once sat. If anyone had seen or heard from Wendy it would be Wendy's half-sister, Sylvie. As his eyes darted between his phone and the black smudges still streaking the marble countertop, his last conversation with Sylvie muscled its way back into the fore regions of his brain. There her words skulked between hazy patches of light, as bristled and as sharp as when they'd followed the slipstream of her lips, pooled among the dust webs enshrouding her living room ceiling, and bore the living, breathing monsters of his waking nightmares.

"For a year she was completely out of her mind," Sylvie had said, lighting a cigarette and offering one to him, forgetting, or never realizing, he didn't smoke. "We thought all that was behind her, as I'm sure you did. She just wasn't the same Wendy I grew up with after starting at that topless place out on Highway 11—the one with the neon rooster. And marrying that lowlife Jimmy Watson didn't make things any better. We'd never seen her act that way. Hell, we'd never seen *anyone* act that way. One minute she was lovable ol' Wendy and the next she was somebody we didn't know, like a switch was thrown, or an alarm went off. She really circled the drain that year, and when she hit bottom she hit hard. But hey, she got through it. She pulled herself together, did her time, paid her debt, and straightened herself out. But we thought all that was behind her. Hoped so, anyway."

"Topless place?" he'd asked incredulously, mouth agape, head swimming, body numb. "Jimmy Watson? And when you say 'did her time'?"

Back in the master bath he shaved, brushed his teeth, combed his hair, and dressed for work, comforted by the familiarity of this portion of his routine, never mind the promise of ten-plus hours (more if he were lucky) of spreadsheets, flowcharts, invoices, and schedules. Probing the dark, puffy semicircles blossoming beneath his eyes, he spotted along the mirror's beveled edge the framed collage made from several years' worth of his and Wendy's vacation photos – Wendy's sturdy, elegant neck cloaked in mounds of cinnamon hair like brittle, wind-swept beach grass; her downward-curving lips the color of a Sloe gin fizz; her supermarket sunglasses reflecting a younger, clearly more naïve version of himself against a placid curtain of blue.

The longer he stared at the collage, even in reverse, the stronger became the notion that should he pass Wendy on the staircase, in the street, or even at the plant, he would no longer recognize her. Accompanying this feeling came the image of a woman on one of those "before and after" drugs posters he'd seen in every park, shelter, and bus station. Facing the collage, he concentrated on Wendy in those same sunglasses cradling a mug of hot chocolate: a day at the lake and a cloudburst that sent them shivering into the nearby marina restaurant. He convulsed as though the icy gales and dime-sized raindrops of that freak summer storm were buffeting him now.

3:30 again and just enough time to grab a sandwich at Weinel's across the street and cruise the vacant lot at the corner of Seraphim and Vine where, days earlier, he'd learned addicts liked to congregate. The first shift managers seldom complained anymore if he was late. What was ten minutes when he'd easily give them ten hours?

Or he could call in sick. With flu season hitting so early this year, every shift, it seemed, contained fewer and fewer healthy employees. The previous night alone he'd sent two home after they threw up in the breakroom and hallway respectively. After that, who would doubt he was genuinely ill? Who at the plant would ever imagine he was instead touring junkie town and rotgut row, parking his car several blocks from his home, and waiting alone in his pitch-black kitchen to give his drug-fucked wife twenty dollars that she might refrain one more evening from emptying their condominium?

Placing two slices of bread in the toaster oven, he froze. What if he called in sick, waited here tonight, and Wendy, as usual, showed up? Should he pretend nothing is wrong? Strike up a conversation as if the past twelve weeks never happened? And how should he react if she wasn't alone? Worse yet, what if the door opens and it wasn't Wendy at all? For all he knew she'd overdosed weeks ago, lost her key, or bartered it for God knows what.

These scenarios and more jabbing his aching brain, he hastily smeared the freshly-toasted bread with cream cheese and two swipes of sun-dried tomatoes—just the way Wendy liked them. Leaving both on the kitchen table, he opened his wallet, and swore—only twelve dollars left.

Praying it would suffice, he tucked the wrinkled ten and two crisp ones under the coffee mug from Boca Raton, inspected the kitchen, and wondered what next would go. Coffee pot, microwave, or toaster oven? Maybe the little television in the corner?

On a whim he opened the cabinet beneath the black smudges where the radio once lived, chagrined to find the glossy black stand mixer gone as well. It had cost a pretty penny, he remembered, even on sale, and he wondered why he hasn't looked for it until now. They'd need it soon for sausage balls, and those miniature quiches everyone at the plant loves. That, and Wendy never shared with him her great-grandmother's recipe for pierogis. She never even wrote it down.

He would hit a couple of pawn shops on his way to the plant, and a couple more tomorrow, he promised, buttoning his coat all the way to his throat, while outside the blanket of gray chasing the retreating sun wavered somewhat, the long shadows of dusk fading as the world was bathed, however briefly, in subtle, amber overtones edged with gold.

As ive imagined your flight to fallujah

Mark Kinnaird

With a single word it has begun
you feel the beat of the blades through the ground
coming steadily
you feel like you've been waiting
all your life for something like this
the sound of the rotor the soundtrack to your emotions
it whips the feelings inside to the surface
they all meld into a peaceful rage
the sand whipping your face
the way a penitent sacrifices his body to his god
shocked to see your emotions on the faces around you
you know that this is one of those moments
the old men have told you about
a moment that will never escape you
a moment that will make you who you will be
a moment when the child slips into the past
as you get closer the tempo rises steadily
and it comforts a faraway place in you

a small island of peaceful waters and skies that go on forever
other emotions a furnace that can't be dampered
fear has oddly mixed with excitement
a new experience
a high that will be hard to duplicate back home
the confidence of youth tells you
youre never going to die
youll live forever
maybe the memories will haunt you
but youll carry them like the medals on your chest
small hesitant steps stretch into strides
and then running towards your rubicon
once crossed life can never be simple again
and you wonder what your friends are doing back home
and wonder if any of them will ever know the feeling
of running towards a place in their own history
you carry a weapon in your hands that was made to kill
men
not to defend a home
or feed your family
but to defend your life and those about you
and the old saw
"a marine prepares for war, but prays for peace"
suddenly make absolute sense
and memories come to you of when you were a child
and the smell of mom's cooking
and the feel of your own bed
contrasted to the spartan life you now know
the closer you get to your objective
you see the faces of your comrades
an absolute mirror your looking into

you know that when this is all over
youll toast friendships forged by this new fire
or you may have the demons of war
that have haunted men for eternity
but you know that it has to be done
you know that you're willing
the spirit is stronger than the flesh
and that you stand united and will never fall
when you take that step up and soon the ground is far below
you are soaring among the heavens
the battle is moments away
you now know that history is made of a moment in time
when you have no where to go but forward

Tobacco Field

The Book of Your Heart

Virginia Smith

Putting up the Christmas tree at my house is a very special event. I relish the ritual of hanging the ornaments I've collected over the years. Each one holds a memory. The shiny silver bell engraved with our wedding date. The brightly painted teddy bear with the year of my daughter's birth painted on his hat. The skiing Santa I bought on our first ski trip. As I lift each treasure carefully out of the box where it has lain hidden from view all year, a precious memory emerges from deep within my heart and finds a place on my tree.

I imagine stories are like those ornaments, each one a treasure nestled within the heart of a writer, waiting to be brought out and displayed. Perhaps that's how we first recognize that we are fiction writers: fictitious people walk and talk and breathe within us, and we burn with the desire to show them to others. A story unfolds with startling clarity in our minds, and we know — just *know* — that we won't have a moment's peace until we've set it down on paper and shared it.

That burning desire is exactly what enables us to tell a story that stirs the imaginations of others. It is our passion for the story and the characters that causes us to spend hours striving for the precise word or the perfect phrase to relay the vivid images in our heads. For some, the stories conceived in our hearts burst from us full-grown; others hold a story inside, nurturing it in the deep places until it ripens into the thing of beauty we've envisioned.

Many years ago, a story bloomed in my heart. It was full of adventure and love, and infused with hope—truly, a thing of beauty. I wrote the first draft feverishly, the words pouring onto the page as the plot unfolded in my mind. The characters were *so* real, their struggles painful and vivid. I studied the craft, intent on telling my tale with artistry. With each new skill I learned, I revised and polished until the story sparkled. If ever a story was born from the heart, it was that one.

Unfortunately, I couldn't find an editor who shared my passion. Whether due to my lack of skill or the uncertainties of the market for that genre, the story of my heart was rejected over and over. I mourned. I raged. I cried out to God, "Why did You give me this story if You don't intend me to tell it?" After my rage died, I revised and polished the manuscript again. Finally, when there was not a single word that hadn't been scrubbed until it shone, I gave up. After all, if there was no place for the story of my heart in the publishing world, maybe there was no place for me there either.

That's when I heard God's whisper: *Do you think I have only one story to give?*

A few days later, a character waltzed into my mind and began telling me about her life. She became real to me, as real as the characters in my first story. I discovered that there was room in my heart for her, too. In fact, this new tale took on a glimmer and shine all its own. I employed the skills I'd honed on my first, and eventually, God placed a published book in my hands.

And then He said: *I have more stories to give you.*

Can you imagine anything sadder than a Christmas tree with only a single ornament? Or a life with only a single precious memory? Or a heart with only a single story?

I am convinced that good stories are born in the heart of God, a heart immense and overflowing with creativity. He carefully selects an author for each one and bestows a precious gift – straight from His heart to ours. We write it and polish it and, when the story has become as beautiful as we can make it, we must hang it on the tree and reach into the box for another treasure.

Tree on the Old Capitol Lawn

January, Early Morning

Pamela Hirschler

The snow clings
in cotton tangles
balanced
on shivered branches.

A robin spins crystal
threads on a cold spindle,
weaves
a thick blanket

on fallen peach tree limbs
over wintered strawberries —
the night empties itself of dreams.
I rise

with the cardinal song.
A hint of sunlight
brushes the dogwood while I await
my lover's return.

The Compliant Child

Pamela Hirschler

Her fingers
stained, bruised, sore by end of day

the growing pile of purple hulls
on a Sunday paper in the grass

plenty of time
for the peas to mound
in the aluminum tub

plenty of time
for the chair to web
the backs of her legs

plenty of time
to think
as long as no one knows

plenty of time
to watch
the spider weave

plenty of time to dream,
but not too much.

Sister of the Brotherhood

Ginny Patrick

A Novel Excerpt

Prologue

Exhaustion tugged at Lisette's eyelids. She must listen, or Jerolin would chastise her later for not paying attention to the Foretelling. But the babies, a son and daughter of the same birth, had been up most of the night and she was too attuned to their infant minds to sleep through their cries. Though the wet nurse had been on hand to care for them, Lisette insisted upon taking her turn pacing the floor, trying to coax the newborns back to sleep. She clamped her teeth together to suppress a yawn and fixed her eyes on the scene before her.

Gathered around an open area in the center of the room, a dozen or so well-dressed men fixed their attention on an old woman with a face like a prune. The Seer, chanting in a low, coarse voice, unfastened the wrapping from one of two bundles and withdrew a gnarled staff the length of her own leg. She tapped the staff gently, dislodging the excess powder, then turned to the first infant. The staff passed slowly over Lisette's sleeping son once, twice, thrice, while the chanting grew soft, then loud, then soft again. As the staff completed its third pass the old woman dashed it to the floor. One of the watchers jerked at the clatter. Blue powder scattered, and the rod rolled a short distance across the polished flagstones before coming to a stop.

The old woman knelt beside the powder, careful not to touch it, and peered at the pattern through half-closed eyelids. No one in the room dared to breathe, lest they disturb her.

Lisette glanced at her husband. Jerolin stood with his hands resting on a narrow table, a wine goblet before him. His jaw bulged as he watched the Seer, though occasionally he glanced toward the other men in the room as though to assure himself that everyone was attending to his son's Foretelling. His guests, in town to witness tomorrow's Naming Ceremony, all gave proper attention to the ritual.

When she finished her examination of the powder, the woman straightened and turned to face Jerolin.

"The child will come to adulthood strong and healthy." Rheumy eyes fixed on a point somewhere above his head. "He will wear his father's name with pride and add to the wealth of that name. I see opportunities in his life never before available to his bloodline. He will touch three crowns, though none will be his to wear."

The Seer bowed her head. Loud applause burst from the onlookers, and the men flanked Jerolin to clap his back. A successful Foretelling.

Three crowns. Lisette smiled and dipped her head at the congratulations offered to her as well. What could the message mean? Perhaps her son would serve three of this kingdom's monarchs, which may portend either a long life for him or short ones for the kings. Or might they be kings from three different kingdoms? A disturbing thought, though Lisette sensed nothing but pride in her husband's mind. Jerolin was not frustrated at the lack of information in this Foretelling, as she was.

She stifled a sigh. That was the problem with prophecies. Too often they merely hinted at the future, and interpretations varied widely from person to person. A reputable prophet never interpreted, thereby avoiding unpleasant consequences. And accountability, as well.

"And now my daughter." Jerolin gestured for the servants to clean the powder from the floor.

Lisette signaled for the wet nurse to take the boy to the nursery, and the stout woman bundled the sleeping infant away. The remaining babe slept soundly in her basket, angelic in appearance. Lisette suppressed another yawn. This same child had not been so angelic in the early hours of the morning, when she should have been letting the household sleep.

When every speck of powder had been cleared away, the Seer took a staff from the second bundle. Lisette watched the rod pass over the babe, while the same mysterious chanting echoed in the chamber. Again, the staff clattered to the floor. This time it rolled farther than the last, leaving a trail of powder on the floor the length of a man.

The old woman cocked her head and hesitated before she knelt. Her glazed eyes moved as she inspected every segment of the design, and then repeated her perusal a second time. From her position on the floor, she lifted her face toward Lisette. The prophetic distance in her eyes dissolved, leaving behind an intensity that stopped Lisette's pulse. Something was wrong. Though the woman's outward posture changed not at all, urgency rolled off the Seer in waves. Lisette sent her inner awareness forward, and the old woman's thoughts whispered in her mind as clear as her own.

The babe's life is forfeit unless her mother acts. But to warn the mother is to also warn the father, and to do that is to kill the child.

Breath lodged in Lisette's throat. Fear saturated the woman's mind. Bound by her prophetic gift to speak the truth, she could not hide any part of the child's Foretelling. But Jerolin's temper was well known.

The onlookers became restless. Jerolin fidgeted with his goblet, his gaze fixed on the Seer. Finally, the woman stood and adopted the same stance as before. Amazing that she could exhibit such control given the strength of her fear. Lisette doubted she could manage to look so calm.

"If this little one lives, her childhood will be lonely, but with great accomplishment at the end. The fate of many will rest on her choices and her abilities. I see crowns near her as well."

The piercing blue gaze lowered, and the woman looked directly into Jerolin's face. Muscles in Lisette's stomach tightened into knots.

"My lord, this babe will bring about the downfall of your bloodline. Because of her choices, your name will end with her generation."

Someone gasped, and every gaze fixed on Jerolin. An

angry flush suffused his face, and his hands drew into tight fists. Lisette heard murder in his thoughts. If she didn't interrupt, the Seer was dead.

She stood and nodded to the nearest guard. "Escort her out and see that she is paid."

The man glanced toward Jerolin, and when he made no move to counter Lisette, obeyed. Visibly relieved, the old woman hurried to gather her empty pouches and scuffled after the guard.

Aware that a dozen pairs of eyes were fixed on her, Lisette walked to the center of the room, took her daughter from the basket and laid her in the arms of a servant.

"Take her to the nursery." She rubbed a finger tenderly across the baby's soft cheek, then turned to face her husband and his uncomfortable guests. "You were right to worry, my lord, about finding a proper Seer in this uncivilized area. This near the mountains, the commoners are poorly bred." The words tasted sour on her tongue, but perhaps tossing Jerolin's own prejudicial opinions back at him would convince him of the prophecy's inaccuracy. "The woman no doubt did the best she could, but she is obviously inept. Perhaps even envious of her betters. I don't believe the Foretelling is accurate."

One of their guests rushed to agree. "She's right, Jerolin." The man nodded with energy. "You should take the child back to the city and have the thing re-told by a prophet with real talent."

Several others murmured agreement, and Jerolin's fists relaxed. At least on the surface, he appeared convinced.

Lisette sent her awareness toward him. His thoughts shouted at her across the room, heavy with fury. *I have my son, what need have I of a daughter? If the girl dies the prophecy will never come to pass.*

Now the meaning of the old woman's thoughts became clear. If Lisette didn't leave tonight, and take her daughter with her, the baby would die at the hand of her own father.

Is this why Lisette had been gifted with the ability to hear unvoiced thoughts? Was this the reason she had known from childhood that she must hide her ability, even from those she held most dear? So that she could save her daughter's life?

As the men followed Jerolin out of the room, a plan began to form in Lisette's mind. In the city she could think of half a dozen people to help her, but here in the country she was days away from anyone she could trust. The villagers in the nearest town were all terrified of Jerolin, and rightly so. She couldn't put any of them in danger by begging refuge. And there was no one in the household she could trust. They were all Jerolin's servants, hand-picked by him and paid well for their loyalty. In the single year since her marriage, she had learned that their loyalty to her was given only because of her position as the lord's wife.

Which meant she must go unaccompanied. And because she was still weak from the double birth, she couldn't take both babies alone.

Pain assaulted her like a knife through the heart. She must leave her son to save her daughter. Her hands clenched, nails piercing the soft flesh of her palms. There had to be another way. A way to take them both. But she could think of nothing.

At least she could take scant comfort in the Seer's Foretelling. The boy would grow to manhood, and provided Lisette did not hesitate, the girl would live as well. When they were adults, their choices would be their own. She couldn't help with those. Her duty was now, and her daughter's need outweighed her son's.

She turned her mind to the details of her escape.

Broadway Street, Frankfort, KY

Crossing the Bridge

Vivian Kelly

Introduction

Good things come to those who wait; I had been waiting for over sixty years to find out the truth about what happened in that Kentucky hollow known as Gayle's Gorge —
what really happened to that young woman. There are those
stories that can never be forgotten. When you least expect,
there they are, the spoken, jumbled words, begging to be put
on paper so the truth will be known.

Chapter 1

It was one of those warm, dreamy Kentucky days in
mid-May, 1955. My mother had run out of sewing thread
while mending dad's work clothes. Her best bet to find
some was our neighbor, Mrs. Rella Montgomery, since Mrs.
Rella sewed all the time. So, the three of us — my young,
beautiful mother; my pudgy, younger sister (three years my

junior); and I, a skinny, seven year old — headed for the Montgomery's house on foot.

My sister and I had long ago thrown our shoes under the bed, out of sight, in hopes our mother couldn't find them. Walking on our dirt-and-gravel road was not a problem for our tough feet. We talked and laughed as children do when they are happy. When we reached the paved road, the warm, smooth asphalt felt so good we danced around and made funny.

"Come on, Vickie. Stop acting so silly, let's get going," our mother scolded me.

A pale-blue sky sported white, puffy clouds that appeared to be chasing each other. Since the roadside daises were in bloom, my sister and I played the old lover's game: pull one petal — *he loves me* and the second petal — *he loves me not*, each of us praying it would end on the coveted *he loves me*.

When we turned into the Montgomery's driveway, my sister and I faced a dilemma — walk or race. With a quick sideways glance at each other, the race was on. It ended with a smack of our bare feet on the cool flagstone of the front porch.

To the right of the cheerful, gray house was an ancient white oak. It provided the house, the yard and family with dense, cool shade. Mrs. Rella and her husband, Mr. Howard, were sitting in their Springer lawn chairs, under the tree, resting — it was just past the noon meal.

"Well, look who's come to visit," he declared.

My mother engaged them in conversation about the weather, their health, and many other things that my sister and I didn't care to hear. So, we moved towards the tree.

"Want to climb the tree?" I whispered to my sister.

She shrugged her shoulders; I took that as a yes. We tried, but that tree was just too fat to get our small arms around. We decided to check the robin's nest we had seen last week; the mom was still on her eggs.

As we wandered back to the adults, I caught the last of Mr. Howard's words—something about going to Carlisle. I liked to go; it made no difference which way the vehicle might be headed. So I eased up to him and pleaded with my eyes.

"Do you want to go?" he asked softly.

I nodded my head in the *yes* direction and bashfully lowered my gaze.

"If it's ok, Faye, I'd like for Vickie to ride along with us," he asked my mother.

"We won't be gone long, and I'll make sure she gets home."

Of course my sister had that hurt look on her face, but I didn't care. She was too little, and, at that time of my life, I was not a dependable babysitter.

So we all piled in the old Chevrolet coupe; Mr. Howard cranked her up; the blue smoke rolled. When he stopped at our lane, my sister was not totally crying, but her chin was all dimpled-up and quivering. Sitting in the back seat, I heard mom say,

"You can help me sew the buttons on Dad's shirt."

That seemed to pacify her. As we pulled off on our adventure, I could see mom holding my sister's tiny hand as they slowly walked up the road to our house in the woods.

After a while, Mr. Howard began to slow down the car and signaled with his arm that we were turning left. I thought we had reached the turn-off for Carlisle, but we were heading straight for a house. The car pulled up to a wooden bridge. I looked down at the little creek that ran under it, always searching for another adventure. The boards were not tightly nailed down, and as each board was run over by the heavy car, it reminded me of the clicking and clacking of the keys on a player piano. That was the first time I would cross that bridge.

We came to a stop in front of a small white house. It looked friendly—lots of colorful flowers and shady water maples outlined the yard and held up the wire fence. He parked the car in the shade because Mrs. Rella and I did not get out. As Mr. Howard closed the yard gate, he started removing the sweat-stained fedora he always wore. A slender young woman burst onto the porch, and gave him a hug. Her hair was blonde, like mine. She waved with her whole arm, and her big warm smile was as wide as her slender face. I decided she was baking because her apron was covered with flour.

When he and the lady appeared again, they walked down to the car, hugs were shared and goodbyes were said. She waved farewell to us as we disappeared over the bridge, onto the blacktop, heading for the big exciting city.

"Someone shot her when she was younger, and the bullet is still in her body," Mr. Howard said. "She got shot in Gayle's Gorge."

"Our Gayle's Gorge?" I could hardly believe what I was hearing. By this time I was hanging over the front seat.

"One and the same," he said.

Oh my, I wished I had looked more closely at that woman. I got up on my knees and looked out the back window, hoping to get one last look at the woman with the bullet in her. *Where was that bullet?*

Chapter 2

Gayle's Gorge is in Piqua; I was real familiar with that place. That's where we lived; that's where we went to Overbey's grocery store. But I had never heard about a shooting. That store had many names through the years. But one thing never changed; this building has always been the center of the community. More news could be learned here than from reading the newspaper. When a friend or neighbor had an accident or died, the family called the store. Anyone coming through the door would be told, and they — in turn — would tell someone else. Pretty soon the whole neighborhood was informed or mourning its loss. Neighbors would gather there to do what we called 'loafing.' The men swapped information about farming, played cards and told tall tales; the women talked among themselves.

"Let's go to Overbey's. We need to get out of the house," my dad said one night.

It was cold weather so we rushed for our coats. My sister and I had almost worn the print off the pages of the our Sears-Roebuck winter catalogue — The Wish Book — carefully marking the things we wished would be under the tree come Christmas morning.

That night, I again heard of the mysterious woman with the bullet in her.

When we arrived, my sister and I ran for the store's copy of the Wish Book, both piled into the same chair and continued with our hunt for happiness. Three of our neighbor-men were eagerly awaiting a fourth player for the nightly card game. When dad came in, they hurried him off to the small, square table behind the oil stove. The women never played, but we kids dreamed of the time we could sit in one of those four power-chairs. The men would promise, but the day never came.

The game heated up; voices called out in frustration when the wrong card had been played. It stopped as quickly as it started, and the conquered and the conquerors moved to their favorite storytelling chairs. The women ceased what they were doing in anticipation of what was to come. The oil stove glowed, the room toasty and warm.

The men started telling stories of times gone by.

"That sure was a bad thing that happened up in Gayle's Gorge. She crawled to this very store for help," my dad said.

When the words *Gayle's Gorge* were uttered, I was jerked back from toy-land to the reality of what was happening in the store. The catalog fell to my lap.

"You lost my favorite page," my sister cried.

"I want to hear this story about that woman," I replied.

All the other men bobbed their heads up and down, or wagged them side-to-side in solemn agreement, mumbling in unison a confirmation as to the un-believability of the event.

"Woman still has the bullet in her," he added.

She crawled to this very building? She was hurt real bad, since she couldn't walk. But I saw her walking, my mind raced.

Just then the metal latch on the door opened and in walked a customer. This loud, metallic click drew my attention away from the conversation. The lady who came in had some kids my age, and I was craning my neck to see if they were with her.

Then I remembered what the men had been talking about. By this time, they had changed the subject of conversation to coon hunting. I got up and approached my dad.

"What did you say about that woman getting shot?" I asked him.

"Go sit down honey. I'll tell you later."

By the time we pulled behind our house that night, my sister and I were asleep in the backseat. So I didn't ask about the story, but the woman with the bullet in her lingered in my mind.

Chapter 3

Retirement gave me free time to accomplish one of my life-goals—I wanted to write. My husband and I ended up in Frankfort, so I enrolled in writing courses at Kentucky State University.

One night, at the beginning of the 2015 spring semester...

"The goal for the Creative Nonfiction class is to write about, in your own words, a true incident. You can embellish, but it must be truthful," the professor said.

The first thing that came to mind was about the woman who had been shot in Gayle's Gorge.

Maybe, just maybe, I thought, *this would bring about the end of the mysterious story. Maybe, just maybe, I would find out why this story had haunted and stayed with me for all those years.*

I actually had no idea of the year it happened; I did not know the names of the participants; I had the unknowns; I needed the knowns. Research started the very next day.

I called a farmer in the community where I grew up. Even though he knew everyone and their stories, he seemed to be drawing a blank about a woman being shot in Gayle's Gorge.

"Bud, she lived in that log house in Ellisville," I tried to stimulate his memory.

"Why didn't you say that? I knew her husband. The last name is McClanahan," he said, "but I don't know her first name."

Near the end of the our conversation, he added,

"Oh yes, I forgot to tell you, her daughter still lives in that house."

Would the daughter of the woman with the bullet in her even want to talk about her mother's ordeal? How would I make contact?

Research was fast and furious. I interviewed — by phone and face-to-face, wrote letters to those that might know, read articles in old newspapers, and used the internet and the State Library and Archives.

"Yes, I remember when that happened. I was nine years old. It was a lover's quarrel. The girl's name was Bernice Montgomery; the boy's last name was Miller, but he had a funny first name and I don't remember it," a long-ago neighbor, now ninety-four, told me. "Why don't you ask his first cousin? We were classmates, and he still lives in the county. Don't you remember him? He ran the hardware store in town."

Then I received an email from the cousin. It said:

"Pearl Miller was a good boy. I just think he got a bad deal."

Chapter 4

Pearl Miller and Bernice Montgomery had been dating for over a year. Bernice first met him when he briefly dated her younger sister. The sister and Pearl were classmates. Even though Bernice was three years his senior, he had asked her out.

"Bernice, let's go for a drive," he said as they left her house.

They walked down to his car, a Chevy roadster. Pearl pulled out a cloth from behind the seat, and started polishing a speck of dust on the fender.

"Why are you doing that? You can already see your face."

"This is my baby," he answered, with a look of pride that boasted he was one of the few young men in the county that had a car like this.

"Let me drive. You know I am a good driver."

He had taught her to drive on the straight stretch of road between Blue Lick and Piqua. She had been a quick study when learning the clutch.

He didn't let just anyone drive his car, so he hesitated for a moment.

"I guess so, since you are going to be my wife," he winked.

Surprised, she jerked her head around, "What are you talking about, Pearl? I have to finish school first."

They often went to the Johnson Creek Covered Bridge. There they shared kisses, and one day they carved their initials on the wall like other lovers had.

"Bernice, I really want to marry you. I know I dropped out of school, but I have a car and a tobacco crop. I can provide for us. You don't need to finish school," he told her.

"But Pearl, I want to finish school. I want to be a teacher."

Pearl took out a pack of Lucky Strikes. He had mastered a new routine with the lighter and hoped it would impress Bernice. He pulled out the new Zippo. It was the "click" of the top opening and closing that thrilled him. As he exhaled, he stole a glance at her to see if it had worked.

But Bernice had been looking at the initials on the wall, trying to identify some of the lovers.

"Well?" he asked.

"I just want to finish school, Pearl. I just want to finish school.

Pearl got a new pistol; it suited his style. Like his car, he kept it spotless. Pearl loved pretty, eye-catching things. That's one of the reasons he wanted to marry Bernice Montgomery. He wanted this pretty thing for his own.

One day he took Bernice to show her just how good he was on the draw and at hitting targets with his new toy. He had placed the cans exactly ten inches apart. He hit all but one.

"Just one time, please?" she begged to shoot the pistol.

He set up the cans again, reloaded the gun and handed it to her.

"Be careful, Bernice," he cajoled.

Bernice hit every can, and then she yelled, "Throw one up in the air." She hit it dead-center.

"Where did you learn to shoot like that?" he growled at her.

"My brothers taught me, Pearl."

Chapter 5

Monday, April 6, 1936

Bernice Montgomery's morning was no different than the previous Monday. The rooster, Big Boy, crowed in the chicken yard; people stirred in the house. The scent of sugar-cured bacon teased her out of a wonderful dream. Her window was slightly open. She loved this window. Through it she could see the farmland she cherished; she could imagine the future; she enjoyed listening to the sounds of the country nights and early mornings.

It was the week before Easter. Bernice had made a beautiful new dress for Sunday. The pastor had asked her to write and direct the childrens' Easter program. She had a very good feeling about this program. The idea had come from something her grandfather, Elbert Suanders Montgomery, had said one time; it tied in perfectly with the meaning of Easter.

She knew her mom would be making biscuits and gravy to go with that bacon. This propelled her to get up and get moving. Today was a school day. In a little over a month, she would graduate as valedictorian of her senior class at Deming High School in Mt. Olivet. *One more test* she thought. It had taken a lot of hard work to achieve this, but she really wanted it. Bernice bounced down the stairs to enjoy the hearty, country breakfast with her family.

"We know where you will be all day, Bernice, but will you be working after school? Will you need a ride home?" her dad asked.

"I'll be working, but I don't need a ride. We girls are walking home together," she answered, looking at her sister.

Bernice gave her mom a kiss, called for her sister to hurry up and ran out the front door. The school bus would be here soon, and for certain, she didn't want to miss it.

Events around the Miller farm were on schedule that Monday morning. There's a rhythm to farming and Charlie Miller and his son Pearl had that rhythm. They had already plowed the tobacco ground; the two men had alternated walking behind the plow. Just holding onto the handles took all a man's strength.

After the noon meal, while the two men cleaned the tools in the shed and greased that plow, they talked farm business.

"Been thinking about new harness for the horses, if the tobacco does good. What you think, Pearl?" Charlie asked his son.

Charlie had to ask again.

"I don't care," he mumbled.

"What's wrong with you, Pearl? Something eatin' at you?" his dad asked.

But Pearl didn't want to talk and Charlie dropped the subject.

While Pearl smoked one of those machine cigarettes, Charlie rolled his own. His favorite tobacco was Bull Durham.

Pearl tapped the pack against his thigh, lining them up, like he had seen the guys do in the movies. He pulled the thin red tab that released the cellophane paper from the top of the pack. A gentle tap against his fist was enough that three cigarettes came out, in a stair-stepped pattern, just like the advertisements.

Charlie loved watching his son go through these graceful motions. *It's almost pretty,* he thought.

"I wonder what they do to this tobacco to make it smell and taste like this. It sure don't smell this way when it leaves our barn," he thought out loud.

Pearl looked at the shadows outside the barn. It was time to go.

"Dad, I gotta' go to Mt. Olivet to see someone," he told his dad.

"That's okay, Pearl, if you have to. The kids will help with the milking. Just be careful and be home for supper," he advised his son, "You know your mom's rules."

He cranked his car. It purred like a kitten. Besides Bernice, it was the most important thing in his life. He had raised tobacco on the halves with two farmers in order to buy it. He felt with his hand to make sure the pistol was under the seat. Last night he had loaded the revolver with seven bullets and put it in his car so his dad wouldn't see him with it. His father frowned upon any kind of gun expect those used for hunting.

At the end of school, Bernice crossed the street to her after-school job at the creamery. She had this job to save money for college. By the time her sister and a friend showed up, the equipment was clean and the cream was ready for pick-up the next morning. The three girls started the walk home.

They heard a vehicle coming on the road behind them, but didn't look to see who it was. Their mothers had taught the girls this would not be proper. But the vehicle started slowing down and when it did, Bernice knew the sound of that engine.

"It's Pearl," she said with a smile.

The car stopped. "Need a ride?" he asked.

"We only have a little ways to go," Bernice told him.

"Come on girls, it's faster.

There's not enough room in your car for all of us," Bernice said.

"Get in," he demanded.

Bernice got in next to Pearl; the other two girls doubled-up on what was left of the seat.

He made a left onto Wolf Run Pike, the road Bernice lived on, and headed for the Montgomery house. He stopped to let the other girl out at her house.

"I'm going to see the new puppy," Bernice's sister said, "Tell mom I'll only be a few minutes."

Pearl drove past Bernice's house.

"What's going on?" she demanded, "I'm tired and have homework and chores."

"I need to talk to you, Bernice."

He didn't say anything right away, just drove. The car slowed down.

"Would you hold the steering wheel while I light a cigarette?" he asked her.

She kept her eyes on the road. This irritated him. He leaned over…

"I want to marry you and I want an answer," he demanded.

There was no reply.

"Bernice!"

"I want to graduate. I'm going to college," was her answer.

He turned right.

"Where are you going? Take me home," she raised her voice.

When he finally stopped, they were in the middle of the

covered bridge; they were miles from her house. It was almost dark.

"What's going on with you, Pearl?"

"We are getting married this week," he glared at her.

She turned her face away from him. She looked at the wall, at the lover's initials; she began to cry. The sides of the covered bridge closed in on her. She could hear Johnson Creek below. They had crossed this bridge many times; it had always been a wonderful place. Still looking at the wall…

"Take me home. Please take me home," she said calmly.

He cranked his beloved car and took off so fast Bernice was afraid. And so, they crossed the bridge.

Pearl drove recklessly, like a maniac.

"My mom and dad will be so worried," she tried to make conversation to calm him down.

Finally she saw the outline of the Piqua Christian Church and the cemetery on the opposite side of the road. *Pearl and his family worship there*, she thought.

Seconds later, the car veered left onto Kentontown Pike. They passed the country grocery store. The lights were on; *it must be seven*, she thought. Her heart pounded in her chest.

"Take me home," she screamed at him, "Take me home."

He slammed on the breaks, bringing the car to a sliding stop in the gravels. They were in the mouth of Gayle's Gorge. He eased the car forward, just far enough so it couldn't be seen from either direction.

"I've got to fix the headlight," he told her.

As he got out of the car, he reached down and quickly brushed the holster with his hand, just to make sure. She watched him go through the motions of doing something to the left headlight. He returned to the driver's seat.

"You are going to marry me by sundown tomorrow. If you don't, it won't go good for you," he threatened her.

She turned to look at him, and from the reflection of the lights, she saw something wild in his eyes.

"Take me home," she demanded, her body visibly shaking as she quickly shifted her gaze to the floorboard.

"I guess we might as well end it all," he said with finality.

"Are you breaking up with me?" she asked, keeping her eyes glued to the floorboard.

He pulled the pistol from under his seat. Bernice noticed this movement out of the corner of her left eye. When she saw the pistol — the pistol he had let her shoot....

"Stop, Pearl. We can work this out," she begged.

But what she saw was a bright flash. She never heard the noise. She was knocked unconscious, her body leaning on the door. The bullet entered directly under her left eye and traveled into the orbit of the right eye, lodging in her skull.

Just a moment earlier, Pearl thought he was doing the only thing that could be done. When he saw the blood running down her face and body, he panicked.

Bernice started waking up. She heard him whimpering and talking to himself, but she did not move. She thought he might shoot her again.

"I will never hurt you again," he said with sorrow.

There was a loud explosion as Pearl put the gun to his chest and pulled the trigger. He slumped over the steering wheel.

"Oh dear God," Bernice screamed, "What have you done?"

She could barely see; she could feel warm sticky blood all over her face and on her clothes.

Pearl has made a complete mess of things, she thought. She was mad at him. Somehow, this anger gave her strength and determination to get help.

We need help; I'm the only one that can go. I can drive the car, she thought.

So she got out and walked around to Pearl, touching the metal with her hand to guide her. She felt faint, but kept telling herself, *I have to do something.* She touched him so gently and tried to talk to him; there was no response. She pushed on his left shoulder hoping to move him from the driver's seat. She tried so hard, but his body just leaned over to the right.

Almost certain that he was dying, she decided to walk to the community store they had passed just minutes before. She was sure it wasn't far.

But how will I get there?

One of her grandfather's stories came to her. He had told her about finding his way home in the dark by listening to the sound of his feet in the gravels. That way he would know he was on the road.

Carefully she put one foot in front of the other. She listened for the crunch of gravels under her feet. Several times she fell. She crawled. She passed a large empty building on the right. Finally she saw soft yellow light from the windows of country store.

Before she collapsed, she saw some men, sitting on the front-porch benches. When they finally saw her staggering into the light, they could not believe what their eyes were seeing. There, in front of them, was a young woman with blood on her face, hands and clothes.

"What in God's name has happened to you?" the men voiced, almost in unison.

Quickly and carefully they helped her inside the store, where they hoped to identify her and find out how she got this way.

"My name is Bernice Montgomery; Tom Montgomery is my father," she told them, "Pearl Miller, the son of Charlie Miller, is in his car at the mouth of Gayle's Gorge. He shot me, and then shot himself. I think he is still alive. Please get help; please hurry," her voice barely audible.

"Doc, it's Chester Wells in Piqua," the owner called Dr. Perry Overbey in Mt. Olivet. "Tom Montgomery's girl is here in the store. She's been shot in the eye. She said Pearl Miller, Charlie Miller's boy, shot her then shot himself. She thinks he's still alive, but in bad shape."

"I'll be right there," the doctor told him.

It seemed like forever, but finally they heard a car roaring down the road. Dr. Overbey gently examined Bernice, and calmly asked her questions while he was doing so. The bullet had entered directly under her left eye. But she was talking and responding in a coherent manner. The bleeding had almost stopped. He bandaged her eyes to prevent further damage from her hands touching her face.

"Load her in the front seat, Chester. Follow me to Gayle's Gorge," Dr. Perry calmly instructed them.

When Dr. Overbey pulled up to Pearl's car, he left his engine running, with the lights on, so he could see Pearl and decide what to do. Pearl's young, muscular body was half-way between the two seats. He moved him into an upright sitting position. Pearl was still alive, but his pulse was very weak. He was unconscious, and he had lost a lot of blood — everything was covered with blood. There was a gunshot

134

wound on the left side of his chest. Dr. Overbey placed a pressure bandage over the wound, wrapping it tightly with gauze.

"Please lay him in the back seat," the doctor told them.

Bernice could hear all of this, but she couldn't see anything. *Dear God, please let Pearl live*, she silently prayed.

"Hey, Doc, we'll wait until the sheriff gets here, and see that nothing is bothered," Chester told him.

Dr. Perry jumped in the car with his new patients, and drove as fast as was possible to his office in town—about five miles.

Chapter 6

The ambulance from Kain and Kessler Funeral Home was waiting in front of the doctor's office. A crowd of well-wishers and onlookers had gathered on the sidewalk. Bernice was further examined and evaluated.

"Take her to the emergency room at Hayswood Hospital," the doctor told the driver.

Pearl was placed on the exam table. His vital signs were not good; he had lost too much blood. Within twenty minutes of arriving at the office, and shortly after Bernice left in the ambulance, Pearl was officially declared dead. It was 8:00 p.m., April 6, 1936.

The Commonwealth of Kentucky Certificate of Death, #12164, stated that Pearl Miller was 15-years 9-months and 7-days old, single, a farmer, died on a public road, by a gunshot wound of left chest, by suicide. Charlie Miller identified the body as his son. On the trip back from the hospital, the same ambulance that had taken Bernice for further treatment, picked up Pearl's body and took it to the funeral home. The next day, he was moved to the Miller's home. Following his funeral at the Christian Church in Piqua, Pearl was laid to rest in the cemetery Wednesday morning, the 8th of April.

Bernice was examined in the emergency room and admitted to Hayswood Hospital. Her condition was stable. The bullet was so close to her optic nerve that the doctor thought any surgery might cause further injury. He said that he might have to remove it if infection or meningitis developed. As it turned out, the bullet remained embedded in her skull the rest of her life.

When the sheriff arrived at the crime scene that Monday night, he found Pearl's pistol and Bernice's bloody schoolbooks lying on the floorboard. Five bullets remained in the chamber. One ended the life of an industrious, reliable young man, widely popular in the community. One changed the life of a young, teenage girl forever.

The incident was headline news. Bernice was not told that Pearl had died. She was in the hospital for eight days. There were daily, front-page updates in the Ledger Independent, keeping readers informed of the young girl's progress. The people in Robertson County, where the shooting took place, were devastated. These were the children of respected families, and no one could come to a conclusion as to why Pearl Miller had done what he did. Bernice's parents put a thank-you notice in the Tribune Democrat, the Mt. Olivet weekly paper, thanking all those that had helped them and their daughter. They did not mention why Bernice was in the hospital. When no infection developed, she was released.

Once at home, Bernice learned of Pearl's death. She began to fear that Pearl's family might try to kill her, because she thought that her refusal to marry Pearl had caused him to kill himself. So great was her fear, she moved her bed away from the window and slept on the floor next to it, especially when the moon was full. Her idyllic life, as it was that Monday morning, when she left for school, was no more.

Bernice was not physically able to attend her own graduation ceremonies. She had been at the top of her class on that fatal day; she graduated salutatorian.

Eventually Bernice would marry and have two wonderful daughters. Active in church, she and her husband both sang in the choir and her little daughters would perform duets. She was an accomplished seamstress, she acted in plays, she worked with her husband on the farm, and despite the injury to her right eye, she became known as "The Annie Oakley of Ellisville" because of her accurate shooting ability. She often demonstrated for her grandchildren how Big Boy, her childhood rooster, had crowed. This earned her the name "Granny Rooster."

Later in life, she became a published author, writing poems and several articles for Kentucky magazines about her grandfather. However, she never wrote about herself or what had happened in Gayle's Gorge. Shortly before her death in May of 2005, she was featured in the Lexington Herald-Leader, in an article—with pictures—about her and the log house where she lived.

Mrs. Rella Montgomery was Bernice's aunt by marriage and a blood relative—third cousin—of Pearl Miller. This was the same woman I rode with that day in 1955, when I first heard about the woman who had been shot in Gayle's

Gorge. Mr. Howard Montgomery was Bernice's uncle, the brother of her father.

Chapter 7

I'm here in front of the bridge. Now concrete, it makes no noise when I cross for the second time. Bernice Montgomery's daughter is giving me an interview. Although I am a few hundred feet from the house, it has taken me many thousands of miles to get here.

She told me about her mother—the woman of Gayle's Gorge legend.

The unknowns had been found; they did not answer why I was haunted by this woman's story. Why such a desire to write this story? Why was the story of this woman the first thing that came to mind? Why did the story unfold for me so quickly—less than a month?

Bernice Montgomery was shot on Monday, April 6, 1936; my writing of this story was finished on Monday, April 6, 2015, seventy-nine years—to the day—since this incident took place.

I believe I was chosen to write the story when I was a young child—when I first heard about the woman with the bullet in her.

The Home

Dennis "Doc" Martin

The sleep haze clears and you stand there, a paper pill-cup
in your hand.
Why did you wake me?
I was fishin' with my dad on the banks of Clear Creek.
Oh? This will help me sleep?
Damn, thought I was, 'til you woke me - for a sleeping pill?

Later that day: "Wake up for your walk."
Why, why, have you once again awakened me?
Don't you realize I was a-runnin' with my future wife
along the banks of Green River?
You say the walk will help my blood flow?
Hell, nurse, pounding hard was my heart 'till you woke
me.

Hello, me again. You ready to eat?
Why, why, why awaken me? I was enjoying the fish!
We fished and ate fried fish back then. It was a way of life

for us.

You wake me now for shredded carrots in orange Jell-O, mystery meat and a roll that could kill a person if I threw it?!!

Wake up! Blood pressure check time!

My damn B.P. is high nurse because you scared me awake!

There he was, football in hand. My grandson was a-runnin' flat out and I was a-yellin'.

What? My BP's high?

Hell yes its high nurse! He ran over 60 yards for a touch-down! My grandson!

Nurse! Nurse! This damn button ain't working, though I push and push.

What? Another break time?

Chest-pain! Damn it hurts! Can't catch my breath!

The nurses, they wake me day and night, but when I need them…

Dad?! Mom! That really you! Look there! Wow! There is…. I have missed

Momma Leebs

Stephen M. Vest

Little Stevie was born into a family of four. When he was 3, his family, which included Mom, Dad, and 18- and 14-year-old brothers, moved to Huber Heights, Ohio, the "world's largest community of all-brick homes."

Little Stevie was a tender child. His arms would pop out of their sockets at the slightest tug. He didn't like the family room couch because it was itchy, and he was afraid of the fescue lawn because it was sticky.

Dad worked at Wright-Patterson Air Force Base and traveled the Midwest and Southeast with the Army Corps of Engineers. Soon Mike, the oldest, who he sometimes imagined was secretly his dad, joined the United States Marine Corps. Shortly after that, Timmy started his freshman year of high school.

"Daddy leeb me," Little Stevie said to Mom. "Mike, he leeb me. Now Tim leeb me."

"Leeb?" Mom asked herself before realizing that what he meant to say was "leave."

"You can't leeb me," Little Stevie pleaded. "Promise, you won't leeb me."

"I promise," Mom said.

More than a decade ago, Mom was in intensive care and not expected to make it until morning. She was in pain from a fall, and Little Stevie, who still lives within me, knew that if he just said, "Mom, it's okay, you can leeb me now," she would have.

But he didn't. He hid away and remained silent. According to Mom, sometime in the night, Dad, who died in 2002, visited her bedside and told her it wasn't her time yet.

The next morning, she was released from the ICU, and after a few weeks in rehab, she returned to the assisted-living facility she called home.

While growing up, Little Stevie and Mom were the best of friends. She worked with him on the double-jointed, rising curve ball that he was sure would land him in the Majors. She explained to him the meaning of the bad words the bullies called him and taught him the correct way to throw a punch. She took him to the doctor when he broke his collarbone and to the hospital when his middle finger was slammed in a neighbor's door.

In the weeks leading up to Mom's death on Memorial Day, she was never alone. Mike and his wife, his daughters and grandchildren, were often at her side, as were me, my wife, and our children. Tim visited from Ohio, and they spent the night telling stories and sharing laughs. Cousins and neighbors and friends from church came by. Mom had fallen. She wasn't eating. She was bruised and weak, but she persevered.

One morning, a housekeeper, who later claimed to be psychic, came into Mom's room and peeked around the corner to Mom's bed. The housekeeper jumped with a start and quickly left the room. When she returned, she apologized and said she was startled by "that man" — pointing to a picture of Dad. "He was here, but she said she wasn't quite ready."

A few days later, the Psychic Housekeeper came in, and Dad was sitting at the breakfast table talking to Mom in the bed. "Marge," he said. "It's time to go." She said, not yet. She said she was still waiting for something.

What? We did not know.

The visits continued. Various people whispered into Mom's good ear, and she often smiled. Mike did. Tim did. Her great-grandson came by with news of his graduation. My daughter, her granddaughter, did, too. Each of her grandchildren took a turn, sharing secrets with granny.

In the midst of the gathering around her bed, I leaned in but had nothing left to say. Mom and I had shared so much over the years. We had no unresolved issues. We loved each other. My mouth opened. Nothing. Children and grandchildren were laughing with one another, and I managed to say, "Look, everything is okay." I paused. My mouth opened again, but it wasn't me. It was Little Stevie. "You can leeb me now."

Mom sighed.

Who whispered what is not important, but when Dad returned in the wee hours of the following morning:

"Marge, are you ready?" "Yes, Harold, I am."

During such times, people often hear and see things that bring them comfort. During my grandmother's funeral, a train passed by with its whistle blowing. My sister-in-law said it was my grandfather, an engineer, who died in 1967, signaling to Mamaw the he was there to greet her. Mom is buried next to Dad at the feet of my grandparents.

During the closing prayer, as if to leave no one in doubt, a butterfly landed on Mom's casket, and the train whistle blew.

Paul Sawyier Public Library

About the Authors

Damian C. Beach is a native Kentuckian, born in Louisville, grew up on a farm in Fairdale where he learned to love to read from his Mother and hard work from his Father. Educated at Bellarmine College (University) he published his first *Civil War Battles, Skirmishes, and* Events *in Kentucky* in 1995. He followed it with *Last Full Measure* in 2012, reprinted *Civil War Battles, Skirmishes, and* Events as an e-book in 2019 along with *Forever Free: An Honor* Roll *of Black Civil War Soldiers Buried in Kentucky.* In 2019 Mr. Beach ventured into the fiction area with *Mother: She's Waiting For You.* Mr. Beach resides in Frankfort and is trying to learn geology.

Terre Brothers is a mother, writer, reviewer, advocate, and editor, with a PhD in sarcasm and a flair for the dramatic. When she is not fighting for peace and justice from her hippie walk-up in Frankfort, KY, she walks between the worlds and speaks to the mist. She learns lots of secrets that way. Her writing reflects her belief that those who are heard the least in this world often have the most to say.

Michael Embry is the author of nine novels, three nonfiction sports books, and a short story collection. His latest novel, *New Horizons*, is the third in the John Ross Boomer Lit series. Embry's interests include writing, reading, photography, hiking, and traveling. He lives in Frankfort with his wife, Mary, and two dogs, Bailey and Belle. Learn more about Michael at www.michaelembry.com.

Keith Hellard is a retired Network Analyst living in Frankfort, Ky. He was educated at Kentucky State University and Eastern Kentucky University. Most recently, he was published in *Trajectory Journal* and is currently writing a novel.

Chris Helvey's short stories have been published by numerous reviews and journals, including *Kudzu, The Chaffin Journal, Best New Writing, New Southerner, Modern Mountain Magazine, Bayou, Dos Passos Review,* and *Coal City Review*. He is the author of *One More Round* (short story collection-Trajectory Press), *Snapshot* (novel-Livingston Press), *Whose Name I Did Not Know* (novel-Hopewell Publications), and *Claw Hammer* (short story collection—Hopewell Publications). Helvey currently serves as Editor in Chief of *Trajectory Journal*.

Pamela Hirschler is a Kentucky native who studied creative writing at Morehead State University and received her MFA in Poetry from Drew University. Her poetry has previously appeared in *Still: the Journal, The Heartland Review,* and *Pine*

Mountain Sand & Gravel. Her first poetry chapbook collection, *What Lies Beneath,* was published in 2019 by Finishing Line Press. For more about Pamela and her work, see her website at www.pamelahirschler.com.

Vivian M. Kelley is a native Kentuckian. Her nonfiction short-story "Make Your Own" received the Richard Taylor Creative Writing Award for 2014, and was published in *The Kentucky River,* 2014. The poem "A Snowflake" was published in *The Kentucky River* 2015. In 2018, her poem, "Even the Grave Can't Bury," was published in *Trajectory.* The Kentucky State Poetry Society published "Curious Child" and "When a Snowflake Falls" in *Pegasus.* Vivian has a BS in Biology and Psychology and MS in Counseling and Psychology from Troy State University, Troy, Alabama. She and her husband are retired and currently reside in Frankfort.

Mark Kinnaird (1959-2019) The coauthor of two books of poetry (*Rebel Angels* and *Yellow Sky*), Mark also authored numerous poems that were published in journals and reviews throughout the United States. In addition to his writing, Mark reviewed books, organized and coordinated book and movie discussion groups, and worked in a public library. At the time of his death, Mark was working on a book of poetry titled *End of Days.*

Dennis "Doc" Martin was born a rural Kentuckian by birth and the grace of God. The son of Kentucky farmers, he

---

writes about his experiences during his youth—for his children and their children. He focuses on writing of a time when the farming way of life was as normal as breathing. Retired and busy now with "Honey Do's and numerous 'Round To Its," Doc now enjoys staying busy at home with grandchildren, community theater, and writing his memoirs.

Linda McAuliffe is originally from Louisville, Kentucky and has lived in Frankfort, Kentucky for 16 years. After retiring from state government in 2014, she is happy devoting more time to writing, reading, and her cats. She hopes to find a publisher soon for her first novel, *Portal of Sapphire,* an urban fantasy. She has been a writer most of her life, beginning with technical writing and more recently branching into creative writing.

Shannon McRoberts writes epic fantasy and urban fantasy books while living in the rolling hills of Kentucky. Shannon is a lover of all kinds of fantasy and enjoys watching her collection of favorite shows like Xena, Buffy, Firefly, Fairy Tail, Game of Thrones, and Farscape. When she's not busy with taking care of her family, binge watching Netflix, or making fantasy art, she is at her computer weaving myths and magic featuring women of grit and steel.

Ginny Patrick is a pen name for **Virginia Smith,** under which she publishes science fiction and fantasy. Writing as Ginny Patrick, she has published one novel and several short stories.

P. F. Powers is a retired middle school Language Arts teacher who enjoys exercise walking, being with friends, being in nature as often as possible, reading good books, practicing yoga, journaling, and occasionally writing poetry. Her poem in this anthology was inspired by the death of her sister in 2015.

Rachana Rahman came to the USA in 1993. Her stories and poems have been published in *Pegasus, The Kentucky River, KUDZU, Best New Writing, Trajectory,* and *Eastern Iowa Review.* Her short story "Fishing Pole" was nominated as Honorable Mention in the 2010 *Trajectory* short story contest and her "China Cabinet" was an Eric Hoffer Award Winner for Prose finalist in *Best New Writing* for 2012. She completed her minor in Creative Writing and major in Computer Science from Kentucky State University and worked for the Kentucky State as a Programmer Analyst. Currently she lives in Frankfort with her husband and son.

Melissa Ann Raine is thirty-one years old and works as a Document Processing Specialist with the Kentucky Retirement System. She grew up in South Frankfort and enjoys walking around the downtown area. It is her life-long dream to be a published author. Currently, she's working on a fantasy series that will be set in Frankfort. She's also begun work on a series of personal essays that will be collected into a memoir.

Virginia Smith is the bestselling author of more than forty novels and many shorter works. Her books have received numerous awards, including two Holt Medallion Awards of Merit. A native Kentuckian, Ginny enjoys introducing readers to the charms of the bluegrass state. Learn more about Ginny and her books at www.VirginiaSmith.org. She occasionally manages to Tweet @VirginiaPSmith, or you can really get to know her on Facebook, where she spends far too much time. Facebook.com/ginny.p.smith.

Richard Taylor, a former Kentucky poet laureate, is the author of 15 books, including two novels, numerous collections of poetry, and several books relating to Kentucky history, the most recent being *Elkhorn: Evolution of a Kentucky Landscape,* published by University Press of Kentucky. Holder of two creative writing fellowships from the National Endowment for the Arts, he is Kenan Visiting Writer at Transylvania University where he teaches English and creative writing. Co-owner of Poor Richard's Books in Frankfort, KY, he lives on a small farm outside of Frankfort.

Stephen M. Vest is the editor and publisher of *Kentucky Monthly Magazine,* which won the Governor Award in the Arts (Media) in 2005. Vest, and fellow journalist Michael Embry, founded *Kentucky Monthly* in 1998 and today it has more than 100,000 readers. He is the author *Unexpected Inheritance* (Butler Books, 2014), two collections of his columns and the publisher of the 2012 anthology *Kentucky's Twelve*

Days of Christmas and the cookbook *Seasoned Cooking of Kentucky*. Vest holds degrees from U of L (1986) and Murray State University (MFA, 2011). His work has appeared in *The Journal of Kentucky Studies and Of Woods and Waters: An Outdoor Reader*. He is also editor of *SAR Magazine*, the National Society Sons of the American Revolution's quarterly magazine. A frequent speaker, Vest is an adjunct professor at Campbellsville University. He and his wife, Kay, reside in Frankfort. They have four children.

Mary Helen Weeks was born July 14, 1946 in Marion County—the county known as "Kentucky Holy Land." She attended Saint Augustine grade school and graduated from Saint Catharine Girls Academy in 1964. She studied at University of Kentucky then lived in Colorado for 48 years. She recently began writing about her Kentucky heritage after returning to KY, "the seat of her soul."

Cove Spring Park

Made in the USA
Monee, IL
28 October 2021